MOCK ROCK:
The Guide to Indoor Climbing

By
Sharon Colette Urquhart

Editors: W. Riefling, Jennifer L. Osborn

Cover Design: Knight Abbey Graphics & Printing, Biloxi MS

Cover Photos: Greg Epperson, photo of Lynn Hill (right)
Beth Laplant, photo of Kingsley Learner

Inside Photos: J. Patrick Cudahy, Peter Kushner

PAPER CHASE PRESS New Orleans LA

100% OF THE PROCEEDS FROM

THIS PURCHASE BENEFIT PROJECT CLIMB

MOCK ROCK:
The Guide to Indoor Climbing

Copyright © 1995   Project Climb/Sharon Urquhart

ISBN 1-879706-63-6: $12.95 Softcover
LC: 94-68861

PAPER CHASE PRESS
5721 Magazine St., Suite 152
New Orleans LA 70115

Printed in the United States of America

For my Dad

He told me I could do whatever I thought I was

big enough to do; you can, too.

DISCLAIMER

Mock Rock: The Guide to Indoor Climbing includes information regarding what you need to know to climb safely in most of America's indoor climbing facilities - **THIS BOOK IS DESIGNED TO SUPPLEMENT (NOT TO REPLACE) INSTRUCTION BY A QUALIFIED INSTRUCTOR.** No book can replace hands-on instruction, common sense and experience. Climbing on any surface is inherently dangerous. Anyone who undertakes the activity should be aware of these dangers, especially if they are inexperienced. However caused, the publisher and/or the author can not accept responsibility for any death, accident, injury, or loss suffered by any reader of this book.

CLIMBING IS DANGEROUS

INTRODUCTION

You have found the tip of an iceberg.

Both spiritual and physical aspects are involved in climbing. Let me explain. The physical part of climbing is probably the most obvious. When you pit yourself against a mountain (or in this case a wall), you use parts of yourself that you might not have known existed. Tendons will stretch, arms will grow more limber, muscles everywhere will become firm. The way your body will respond to you is in direct relation to the amount of commitment you give to climbing.

Spiritually, climbing can transform someone from uncertainty into confidence. When you are faced with multiple decisions about how to reach the top, and you make them successfully, you forget any fear or doubts as you had at the bottom and sheer joy can fill your soul. Climbing can take someone who is not a risk-taker and transform them into a powerful individual, full of high self-esteem, explicitly because climbing involves them as an individual *and* as a team.

Climbing unfolds from there to go outdoors onto real rock in all its diversity, into the commitment of lead vertical climbing and direct aid, trying smaller and larger cliffs, possibly even on to vertical camping on ultimate sized walls like Half Dome and El Capitan. In another direction lies the world of mountaineering, of peaks and summits, of scrambling and climbing ridges, buttresses and walls, of high altitude and cold and weather. Higher in the mountains there is snow and ice to climb on. *Neve,* glaciers and frozen waterfalls, entirely new techniques with ice axe and crampons.

Yet in even those remote realms, the climbing itself still evolves out of the same basic lessons of balance, stance, and movement, the same ropes and belay techniques, the same gradual evolution of fear into respect that you first encounter from your first venture upward indoors.

This toe hold you've found on the world of climbing may be the tip of the iceberg, but it happens to be the perfect place to start. Beginning to climb is never easier, safer, or more convenient than indoors with its elements reduced to their absolute simplicity. Indoor climbing is a picture of innate complexity and contrasts. It requires the use of strength tempered by technique, the attempt to ensure safety in a potentially dangerous environment, and the achievement of a balance between anxiety and determination. As you progress along at your own pace, guided not only by this book, but by experienced climbing instructors, you will feel your confidence level rise, both in the adventure of climbing and the adventure of everyday life. Through efficiency of movement, effective use of energy, and the power of balance, the indoor climber can traverse pathways through the impossible.

Doug Robinson

CONTENTS

Chapter One

ORIENTATION

Climbing is a complex sport in which gym climbing and competitions have become viable aspects. The intent of this volume is to introduce the reader to climbing on human crafted surfaces. Included are the basics which every climber will need to know to climb independently of supervision at most gyms. Hence, this guide may be used as a textbook for courses, or as an informative guide for prospective climbers.

While many facets of climbing are mentioned in *The Indoor Guide to Climbing,* it does not attempt to cover all aspects completely. Likewise, *The Indoor Guide to Climbing* is just that, a guide book. It is not intended for use as a substitute for quality instruction. *The Indoor Guide to Climbing* will prepare you for your first climbing lesson, and will offer reassurance when you're at home practicing your knots. Further, you may refer to it time and again for technique tips, gym locations, or equipment information.

The importance of a qualified teacher and thorough, careful instruction can not be stressed enough. Each year lives are lost because people make fundamental errors. While there is no guaranteed way to prevent accidents, proper training and solid knowledge of basic skills have allowed thousands to climb safely for many years.

Climbing Defined

Climbing on rock walls and on manufactured climbing surfaces like those found at climbing gyms is an exciting and challenging route to fitness. Climbing is about solving the problem of physically getting up a wall or rock. Strength, finesse, flexibility and commitment are necessary in both the body and the mind. Therefore, climbing is accessible to many different types of people - not just the severely fit.

Climbing demands that you take responsibility not only for yourself, but for a climbing partner as well. Trust takes on new meaning when you allow your life to be held in the hands of your partner. Climbing will sever the bonds of some relationships while it builds those of others because it demands trust, responsibility, cooperation and communication.

Lunging For A Hold

So you want to give climbing a whirl but don't know a soul who would ever try it, much less already be into it? Climbing gyms are a great place to start. However, never assume that a climbing school or instructor is competent simply because they are advertising as such. Ask questions regarding instructors including what medical training they have, how long they have been climbing *and* teaching, and whether the organization has liability insurance. Because you will be engaging in a risky activity, you should feel confident about your instructor's competence and the professionalism of the organization they represent.

To climb, one must first be willing to accept the personal responsibility of the endeavor. Even in a rock gym, climbing is a dangerous sport. Like most activities, climbing is only as safe as people make it. Used properly, climbing ropes won't break, harnesses won't fail, and carabiners won't snap. *Most of the accidents and deaths which are climbing related occur because people have failed to use equipment properly.* It is critical to learn the basic safety skills of climbing thoroughly and to learn from responsible individuals or organizations.

Climbing Gyms

Climbing gyms are a convenient place to take a basic safety course. Climbing in a gym is different than climbing in the natural world. While body movements across natural and human crafted surfaces are virtually the same, the environment couldn't be more different.

Climbing Gym Under Construction

Climbing in a gym provides a controlled atmosphere free of rock fall, weather hazards, and strenuous hiking to the crag. Thus, a gym allows the climber to push gymnastic limits and to test ability in a relatively safe and convenient arena. It won't get dark nor will lightening strike at the gym, and a double espresso should always be available! A basic safety course at a climbing gym should cost between $30-50 depending on what is included in the lesson and where it is taught (lessons taught outdoors are often significantly more expensive).

Newly Constructed Climbing Gym

In your first lesson you should learn about your *harness*, how to tie your *knots*, and how to *belay*. Belaying is the process of taking up the rope as a climber ascends and stopping the rope should the climber take a fall. While tying knots and belaying are not complex skills, it is necessary to be totally comfortable with what you are doing and to accept the personal responsibility which accompanies engaging in this high-risk activity. Have fun, take your safety seriously, your coffee with cream, and yourself with a grain of salt!

Chapter Two

CLIMBING EQUIPMENT For The Gym

Climbing in a gym requires that you have certain basic skills and knowledge of climbing equipment. This chapter explains many of the essential aspects of these skills and equipment. You shouldn't have to buy climbing equipment to climb in a gym - you can generally rent anything you need. Eventually you may want to buy your own harness, shoes, and hardware, therefore, this section is written with an eye towards making wise purchases for gym climbing.

The Union Internationale des Associations D'Alpinsim (UIAA) is an international organization which tests and approves tested climbing equipment. Similar to the UL listing which dependable electronic equipment usually has, your climbing equipment may be UIAA certified and the manufacturer will indicate that status directly on the equipment or with accompanying literature. Responsible manufacturers of climbing equipment test their own equipment and generally exceed the UIAA standards for safety.

UIAA Certification/Manufacturer Labels

The Climbing Harness

The climbing harness is a critical link in your climbing safety system. The harness itself must be durable, fit properly, and must be properly used. It is possible to make your own harness, and many climbers do. The advantage is cost, the drawback is usually comfort. The following discussion is concerned with harnesses produced by climbing gear manufacturers, as most gyms require that you use a harness manufactured by a reputable company.

There are three basic climbing harness types, and several different harness styles. Harness types may first be differentiated based on their method of securing: either *tie-in* or *buckle*.

Tie-in harnesses are very safe when properly used, but can be inconvenient in certain situations. The buckle harness is quick and easy to get into, but it is critical that the belt buckle be fastened properly. On American designed equipment this generally means ensuring that the belt is *double-backed* through the buckle. If the belt is not double-backed through the buckle, there is grave potential for the belt to come undone from the buckle, and for the climber to be unexpectedly released from the harness.

The basic harness styles or designs include:

- the *seat*
- the *diaper*
- and the *waist belt* with *leg loops*.

Seat Harness

The seat harness is a one-piece unit, generally unpadded but may be adjustable. The *Yates* brand "Alpine Instructional" harness is a seat harness with adjustable leg loops.

YATES Seat Harness

Diaper Harness

The diaper harness is also a one-piece unit, with the added design feature of adjustable and sewn, but semi-detachable leg loops. Advantages of a diaper style harness includes the ability to drop or adjust the leg loops without ever detaching them completely. The *Black Diamond* brand "Bod" harness is a diaper style harness.

Black Diamond "Bod" harness

"Waist belt with separate leg loop" Harness

The "waist belt with separate leg loop" style harness is popular among sport climbers; it is easy to get in and out of, it can be extremely lightweight, and a sewn *belay loop* is typically included. The *Petzel* brand "Jump" harness is a comfortable choice of this type of harness. *Metolius* sells the leg loops and waist belt separately so you may size them specifically to your body.

Petzel Brand "Jump" Harness

For kids and others with special needs, the use of a chest harness is often appropriate. The chest harness offers additional support and stability for the climber. *Petzel* makes a harness specifically for kids called "Ouistiti," or "Little Monkey" which is a one piece unit. This harness is a great choice for active kids.

The fit and comfort of your harness should be high priorities regardless of what type and style of harness you select. Your harness should be snug but not pinching or binding, allowing for a full range of mobility. Your harness should be lightweight without compromising on durability or strength. Finally, getting in and out of your harness shouldn't feel like an aptitude test - it should be easy to use.

Your harness is an investment in your own comfort, safety, and fun. When you shop, have an idea of what your climbing needs for the next year or so might be. Try on several different brands and styles of harnesses before you buy. Ask others how they like their brand and style of harness - most climbers will be happy to gab about the pros and cons of their gear. Read harness reviews in climbing magazines or at your pro shop. Finally, find out about the company who manufactures your potential harness, and how they test their harnesses for strength. But always remember, safety and comfort is ultimately your responsibility.

CAUTION
YOUR HARNESS MUST FIT SNUG ABOVE YOUR HIP BONES AND ALL BUCKLES MUST BE FASTENED PROPERLY, COMMONLY BY BEING "DOUBLE-BACKED."

Properly Double-Backed Petzl Harness

Climbing Shoes

Climbing shoes fit snug, often tight. They absorb odors like no other shoes you've owned. They never seem to last quite long enough, and they are rather expensive. Despite their drawbacks, those same shoes will take you to places you never dreamed possible. They are an adventure in a box waiting for you to put them on.

Climbing shoes should feel snug, and the most extreme of climbers will wear their shoes several sizes smaller than their street shoes. Look around at the toes you see in the locker room at the climbing gym; bunions, missing toe nails, callouses, and deformities are the standard fare - climbing shoes being the root of these problems.

Your climbing shoes should really fit, well, like a glove. This means they won't be as comfortable as your Reeboks at first, but don't buy shoes too small. Unhappy feet will make for an unhappy climber.

There is a vast range of climbing shoes available, and they can be broken down into several categories: slipper, low-top, boot; lace-up or Velcro; lined or unlined. The *sticky rubber* and their design make them expensive. Annually the climbing magazines do shoe reviews. These reviews are a good place to check for the *beta* on what is available.

Climbing Boot

The climbing boot is a full support shoe which covers the ankle. Boots are generally lined and may have a full *rand*, or the part of the sole which extends around the toe and sides of the shoe.

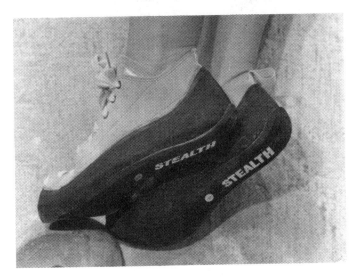

5.10 Brand "Summit" Boot

Low-top

The low-top boot is a trimmed down version of the climbing boot. The low cut reduces support but increases range of motion. The low-top boot may have a partial rand.

5.10 Brand Low-Top Boot

Slipper

The slipper is a flexible shoe with little support making weak feet strong in virtually no time. Slippers may be lace-tied or fastened with Velcro or elastic. Slippers slide on and off with ease, making them a favorite at the gym.

5.10 Brand "Aysem" Slipper

NOTE
PUT BAKING SODA IN YOUR NEW SHOES BEFORE YOU CLIMB AND THEN EVERY TIME AFTER YOU CLIMB.

Chalk & Chalk Bags

Magnesium carbonate and other synthetic chalk-like substances are often used by climbers to absorb sweat on the hands. Chalk may be purchased loose, in blocks, or in refillable chalk balls. It is carried in a cute little bag hanging from a belt. Chalk bags are fun and chalk is cheap. Chalk creates dust, and in many climbing gyms additional particulate matter in the air is intolerable. Therefore, use of chalk is not allowed in some climbing gyms.

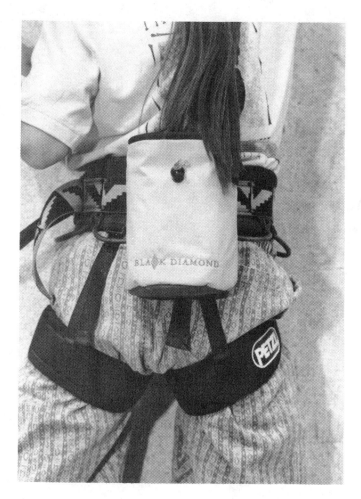

Black Diamond Chalk Bag

The use of chalk outside is also questioned by many for environmental or aesthetic factors. It doesn't really hurt anything, but white chalk on beautiful pink sandstone or dark granite doesn't work visually for many people. Climbing areas may have no-chalk standards, or locals may request that chalk is blended with color to match the rock.

The use of chalk is largely a personal choice, but the obsessive nature of so many climbers often leads to a chalk addiction. Chalking up while driving is commonplace among the afflicted. It is best not to let your chalk habit get out of hand.

The Climbing Rope

The climbing rope is your life line. It must be designed well, handled properly, and meticulously cared for. In all climbing facilities in America today you will find the *kernmantle* type of rope in use. This is a synthetic line constructed with an inner nylon core and an outer, generally colorful woven pattern. Rope strength depends on the diameter and the brand of rope used. Most gyms in America use 11mm ropes cut to proper length for *top roping* on the particular gym's walls. At climbing gyms where you may *lead-climb*, you are generally required to bring your own rope, subject to inspection by gym staff.

To ensure a long and quality life for a rope, proper handling is necessary. Particles of dirt within the rope may damage the yarns by abrasion. Dirt particles may also increase the friction between the yarns, reducing suppleness of the rope. Never step on a rope as it may embed dirt or cause damage to the sheath. The facility you are climbing at should monitor the use and wear of their ropes. If you suspect serious damage to a rope, it is in your own best interest to inquire about the history of the rope, as it may be time to retire it.

In terms of care for your own rope, it is advisable to understand how your rope absorbs the energy of a fall. This information should come with the rope you purchase; if not, ask your sales clerk to provide you with that information for your particular rope.

Careful rope management will also help to avoid unnecessary wear. Sharp edges are extremely dangerous to ropes, and the natural world provides plenty of opportunities for severe rope damage. While gyms are generally designed to avoid such hazards, they may exist.

Quality control of the ropes used at your gym and your personal ropes should be a serious concern. Check your rope for possible damage before and after each use. Sheath damage may be indicative of damage to the core. For safety's sake, you may wish to keep a journal of your rope use. With a written log, you will be better able to judge the condition of your rope. Your climbing gym should have some type of record keeping system for its rope use.

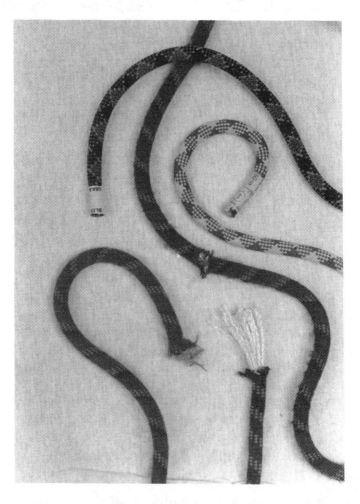

Various ropes in different stages of use

Carabiners

Carabiners come in various shapes, styles and colors, but basically they are snap-links, some of which have locking gates. Carabiners are generally made of light weight aircraft quality aluminum or steel. Steel is significantly heavier than aluminum, but it is also stronger. Weight and strength of carabiners is not as important when climbing in a gym as it is outdoors.

At the gym you will only need one *locking carabiner* - to link the rope to you as it passes through your belay device. Outdoors you might need more than twenty regular carabiners and several locking ones - creating a much heavier *rack* of equipment, especially if they are all made from steel!

The locking carabiner comes in two styles: the *twist lock* and the *screw gate*. The twist lock style is virtually an automatic locking device; as long as it is functioning properly, when the gate of this carabiner is closed, it will close itself. The screw gate carabiner locks manually when the climber screws the lock on the gate shut. Both styles work well, and it is up to the climber to decide which will work best for him or her.

Locking carabiners are also designated by shape; the basic shapes include *oval, D*, and off-set *D*. There are now several hybrid versions of these basic shapes on the market, but an understanding of the basics will take you far. The locking oval and D carabiners are functional, yet not the most desirable for gym climbing. It is the locking off-set D carabiner which is most functional for belaying at the gym.

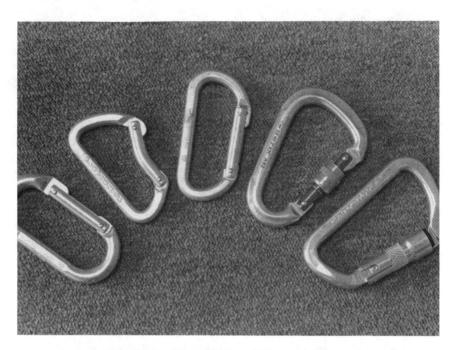

Various Carabiners (left to right):
Oval, Bent Gate, D, Locking Off-Set D, Twist-Lock Off-Set D

The wide end of a locking off-set D carabiner will accommodate the bulk of your harness while allowing your belay device to brake effectively on the narrow end. Oval and regular D shaped carabiners are awkward because they are just not wide enough to accept your harness and the rope for belaying. Select a carabiner only after you have allowed your hands to work with both a screw gate and a twist lock; get the one which works best for you.

Belay Devices

There are dozens of *belay devices* available throughout the world, yet virtually only one way to belay. Hence, it is important to have a grasp of belaying prior to investing any money into a device. Furthermore, every climbing gym has its own requirements about belay devices.

Standard belay devices are made from aircraft quality aluminum. While these devices vary in shape and size, they all work the same way: the rope is pinched through the device and then clipped to the belayer via the locking carabiner.

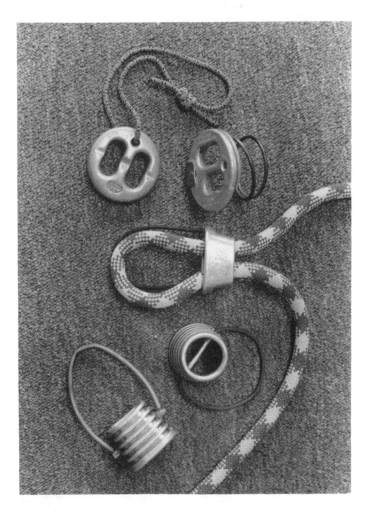

Various belay devices (rope is pinched through the Black Diamond Air Traffic Controller (ATC))

The *active end* of the rope - the climber's end - is either fed out or taken in by the belayer as needed by the climber. When the climber falls or needs to be lowered, the belayer *breaks* by pulling back on the *break end* of the rope. Doing this causes the belay device to lock the rope up against the carabiner, thus preventing it to pass through the device, the carabiner, and the belayer's hand.

The *Grigri* device is used exclusively in many gyms. This is an automatic-locking belay device which can be used by just about anyone regardless of their belay experience. It would seem that all gyms would require this device to be used, but the disadvantage comes in cost - the Grigri is significantly more expensive than standard belay devices.

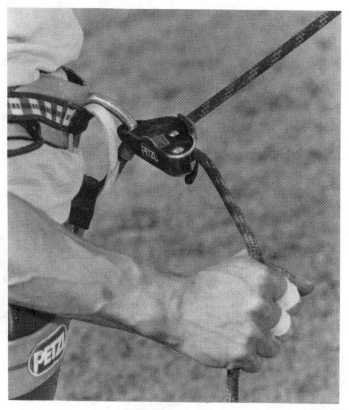

The Grigri

The *figure-8 rappel devices* are UIAA certified for rappelling, but not as a belay device, hence most gym managers will not authorize the use of figure-8's at their facilities for belaying. Furthermore, the *Munther Hitch*, a popular hitch-knot commonly used for belaying in Europe, is also not accepted as a method for belaying at most climbing gyms.

Outdoor Rack (climbing equipment) versus Indoor Rack

Chapter Three

PROPER USE OF
Climbing Equipment

Most of the accidents which happen when climbing occur because of *human* error, not equipment failure. Climbing is dangerous because people get *careless*. Climbing in a gym is generally safer than climbing out of doors because gyms eliminate many of the variables present outside. Nevertheless, if a climber doesn't double-back his harness or *tie-in* properly, he is putting himself in grave danger. Likewise, if the belayer hasn't double-backed her harness, locked her carabiner, or if she takes her break hand off the rope, she is putting herself and the climber in grave danger. While it hasn't happened yet, the potential for a climbing related death in a gym is very real.

The Top Rope System

Top roping is a popular way to climb both at the gym and outside because, when set up properly, it can be quite safe. There are several elements involved: the anchor, the rope, the climber and the knot, the belayer, and the *communication* between the climber and the belayer.

Climbers using Top Rope System

Anchors at the gym should be *bomb proof* - a climber's term for infallibility - there is no reason an anchor at a gym should ever fail. Nevertheless, it is the climber's responsibility to ensure his or her own safety, so examination and inquiry about the anchor systems at your gym is reasonable.

Most gyms use large steel tubing which runs through steel brackets bolted to the framework of the climbing structure. The climbing rope runs over the tube, sometimes the rope is even wrapped around it once to create more friction, and both ends of the rope hang at ground level. The climber will tie-in to one end of the rope, and the belayer will take-up or let-out from the other end of the rope. Thus, this anchor is what holds the rope up at the top of the wall, and what will hold *you* up when you fall or need to be lowered.

Floor Anchor

Lead Climbing

Lead climbing is a more advanced climbing technique and should be attempted only after mastering the basic safety skills for climbing. Lead climbing consists of the same essential elements as top rope climbing with one critical difference: the climber must establish anchor points as he ascends the wall rather than relying on a fixed top anchor. This means that the climber must climb beyond his anchor point to get to the next anchor point. The climber, should he take a fall, will drop twice the distance between his knot and the last anchor point, and a little bit more when the rope stretches. Thus the consequence of a fall becomes more significant while leading. The prospect of lead climbing is terrifying to some, while others seem to have an insatiable drive to ever be on the *sharp end* of the rope.

Jay Weber Lead Climbing

Climbing gyms which have lead areas generally offer some form of instruction for leading. The anchor points will generally be established at gyms: a *quick draw,* or two carabiners with a sling of webbing between them, will be clipped into a *bolt* already established on the climbing wall. All the climber needs to do is clip the rope into the carabiner properly for a safe anchor point.

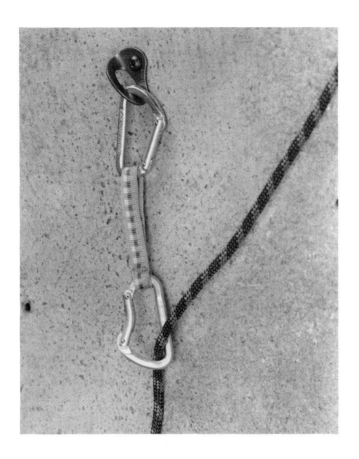

A bolt clipped with a quickdraw and rope

Belaying a lead climber is different than belaying a top roped climber in that the belayer is letting rope out more than she is pulling it in. Belaying a leader should be attempted only after mastering the skill in *ground school.*

Climbing in a gym and climbing outside could not be more different in terms of anchors. Someone has taken great care in the gym to insure that top rope and lead bolts and anchors are *bomb proof*, or extremely safe.

Jacob Weber at the lead anchors

Climbing outside requires the climber to establish anchor points. This may be done with bolts as in the climbing gym or with various gadgets which may be placed in cracks and later removed by the climber who follows the leader. Hence, the safety of the anchor point correlates directly to the experience, knowledge, and sensibility of the climber. Furthermore, anchor failure may occur for reasons beyond human control such as rock fall. That climbing is extremely dangerous becomes evident when one stops to think about anchor points. Never underestimate the ability of the vertical world to spank you.

Knots

Knots are a critical link in the rope. The figure eight follow-through knot is strong and easy to check visually, making it a commonplace requirement for tying in, or connecting the climber via the harness to the rope, at climbing gyms. A double bowline is equally strong and preferred by many climbers, but it is more difficult to check visually and therefore less accepted at climbing gyms. Whatever knot is used, it is critical to *always* check one's knots. Very experienced and talented climbers have taken long falls as a result of not checking their knots. Keep in mind that it is far easier to retie your knot when you're on the ground than it is to notice 30' off the deck!

Knots may be difficult to learn, and they seem to be easy to forget, at least at first. Tying various knots for climbing will eventually come second nature to you, but even then, remember to always check yourself.

The Figure of Eight Follow-Through Knot

To begin, select the end of the rope you'll be climbing on - it should be the one closest to the climbing surface. Look above to see if the rope is twisted - you want the rope to glide smoothly over the anchor.

Prior to tying your knot, check to see if you have put your harness on properly: Is the waist belt snug above your hip bones? Is the buckle double-backed? Proceed only after there is no question in your mind that your harness is on properly.

The figure eight knot is tied first as follows:

1. Grab the end of the rope and pull out 4.5 to 5 feet of rope.

2. Make a *bight* in the rope.

3. Wrap the tail once around the bight, then thread the tail through the bight.

You should end up with a knot which looks like a figure eight - if it looks like an overhand knot or a twisted pretzel, the knot is probably not a figure eight.

Tying a figure eight knot

Your knot should have a tail which is nearly four feet long. To finish the knot, thread the tail of the rope directly into your harness.

This will be different on different harnesses; naturally you will want to know exactly what it means on your harness. The information provided by the manufacturer of your harness will indicate the tie-in point on their product. After you have the tail threaded through your harness, pull it so the figure eight knot is right next to the belt of your harness. You are now ready to finish the knot with the *follow through* part of the knot.

To follow through a figure eight knot, you will trace the knot you have already made exactly, starting from the point at which the rope leaves the harness and forms the knot. You'll trace the first knot with the rope's tail, until you have a perfect parallel match to the original knot. You should end up with a tail of about one foot long.

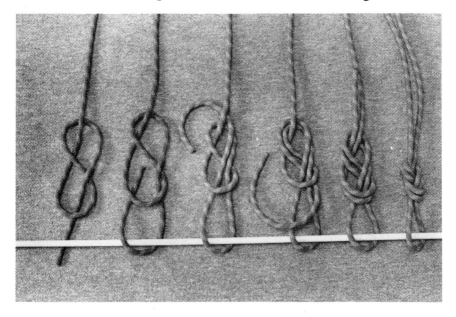

**How to follow through a Figure Eight Knot
(steps shown from left to right)**

When tied correctly, the figure of eight knot will not need a *back-up knot*. Because climbing safely is the goal, a *fisherman's knot* should be used as a back-up knot. The fisherman's knot will tighten up onto itself in the event of an incomplete figure of eight knot. Many climbers would have been saved unnecessary accidents and deaths had they tied a fisherman's knot as a back-up.

The Fisherman's or Back-Up Knot

To tie the fisherman's knot follow this:

1. Take the tail of the rope, and wrap it once, then twice around the rope leading to the anchor, so that the wraps cross to make an X.

2. Take the end of the rope and thread it, starting from the bottom, up underneath where the X crosses, and pull tight.

You should end up with a short tail and a neatly tied fisherman's knot backing up a figure eight follow through knot. The climber is now ready to climb.

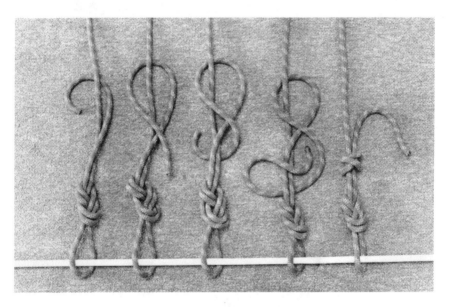

How to tie a Fisherman's Knot
(shown from left to right)

CAUTION
ALWAYS DOUBLE CHECK YOUR KNOTS.

Belay Technique

Belaying is the process of taking up or letting out rope for the climber. Belaying is not a difficult process, but it must be done correctly. In some ways it is similar to rubbing your stomach in circles while patting your head at the same time; a simple task, but one that can be confusing. The belayer must remain aware and competent throughout the entire process to be effective.

Setting-Up To Belay

The belayer's equipment includes a harness, locking carabiner, belay device and the rope. The harness must fit and be double-backed to be effective for belaying. The carabiner is connected directly to the harness via the same points the rope would be tied through for climbing. The rope is pinched through the belay device and clipped into the carabiner which is then locked. Setting up with the *Grigri belay device* requires laying the rope in the device, then clipping it to the harness, and locking the carabiner.

Climbing gyms are often equipped with floor anchors. The belayer may clip into the floor anchor with the same locking carabiner from which they will belay. The floor anchor will keep a lighter climber on the ground while belaying, though it does not ensure a safe belay: that is the responsibility of the belayer.

Double-Check For Safety

To double-check for safety before climbing, observe the following procedure:

1. Is the climber's harness on correctly?

2. Are the harness buckles fastened properly (double-backed)?

3. Is the rope threaded through the right places on the harness?

4. Is the Figure Eight Follow-Thorough Knot tied correctly?

5. Has the back-up knot been tied properly?

6. Is the belayer's harness on correctly?

7. Are the harness buckles fastened properly (double-backed)?

8. Is the carabiner clipped through the right places on the harness?

9. Has the rope been set up properly with the belay device?

10. Is the carabiner locked?

The photo below shows a climber properly tied-in with the harness double-backed and snug above the hip bones. Also, the rope has been threaded through the waist belt and leg loops, and the Figure Eight Follow-Through Knot is backed up with a Fisherman's Knot.

Properly Tie-in Climber

CAUTION
ALWAYS DOUBLE CHECK EACH OTHER FOR SAFETY NO MATTER HOW COMFORTABLE YOU FEEL WITH YOUR SELF OR YOUR PARTNER - YOU MAY SAVE THEIR LIFE OR YOUR OWN.

Communication

Now the communication begins: the climber and the belayer want to be certain that they are ready for the endeavor. The climber asks:

"Belay on?"

This can be used as a cue to the belayer and the climber to check everything one more time. With everything checked out and safe, the belayer responds:

"Belay on."

The climber then indicates to the belayer that he would like to begin by saying:

"Climbing."

Before he leaves the ground, the climber waits to hear the belayers response of:

"Climb on."

This communication is very simple, but it is critical for effective and safe climbing. It gives both the climber and the belayer time to examine themselves and each other for safety. When the climber leaves the ground, belaying begins.

Belaying

The belayer has two hands. One hand will act as the *brake hand* and the other hand becomes the *active hand*. Generally the belayer will use the hand they write with as the brake hand. The belayer pulls rope with the active hand, *in* towards the belay device, while simultaneously pulling the rope with the break hand, *away* from the belay device.

Active hand towards belay device;
Brake hand away from belay device

The active hand pinches both ropes together *above* the brake hand. The brake hand is loosened only enough to *slide* it down the rope towards the belay device.

Active hand pinches both ropes together above brake hand

Braking

To brake, the belayer grips the rope tightly with the brake hand and pulls the rope down towards the hip causing the rope to lock up between the carabiner and the belay device.

Belayer braking

If the belayer opens his brake hand, the braking system will fail. The belayer must keep his brake hand on the rope at all times to be effective.

Lowering

The climber will need to be lowered to the ground once he or she has reached a high point. To do this, the belayer must brake. The climber will sit in the harness, like in a swing, placing the soles of her feet flat on the climbing surface. This can be the hardest thing the climber will do all day because they are yielding all control of fate to the hands of the belayer.

The belayer begins lowering only when the climber is stable. Starting from the **brake** position, the belayer **slides** her hand down the rope. With her hand firmly around the rope, she allows the rope to slowly **suck** through the belay device.

When her hand is near the belay device, she brakes again, slides her hand down the rope and allows the rope to suck through the belay device. Care should be taken to lower the climber smoothly and never too fast.

Rappelling

Rappelling is the glamorous feat often performed in join-the-army commercials: an individual "slides" down a rope from a helicopter or bounces down a cliff side. Rappelling seems as if it would be fun, but ask veteran climbers and many will say it is the aspect of climbing they like least. In the climbing gym you will have little reason to rappel; the belayer should always be able to lower you to the ground. However, rappelling in the gym can be utilized as a tool for learning the skill.

Many of the belay devices available today may be used both to belay and rappel, but cetainly not all of them. It is the user's responsibility to read the information which comes along with their purchase. The set-up for rappelling is similar to that of belaying: a locking carabiner is linked through the strongest points on the harness, the rope will be pinched through the device and clipped into the carabiner. If the rope is anchored at the top, and the climber is at the top, she may anchor herself in, then prepare to rappel.

The major difference between belaying and rappelling in terms of the rope is that in rappelling both parts of the rope must be utilized.

Likewise, both openings in the rappel device must be used (one for each half of the rope).

Rappelling can be extremely dangerous due to the potential of anchor failure and other human error. Therefore, you must never rappel in a gym without supervision and without prior permission being granted by gym management.

Tom Davis Rappelling

More Communication

When the climber wants extra rope to be pulled up by the belayer, she should say:

"Up Rope."

When the climber needs some extra rope:

"Slack!"

When the climber is about to fall:

"Falling!"

When the climber wants to rest or otherwise weight the rope:

"Tension." or "Take."

To alert those below when the climber drops something (even if it isn't a rock) or a hold breaks:

"Rock!"

When the climber reaches their high point:

"Got Me?!"

When the climber would like to be lowered:

"Lower Me."

When the climber is back on the ground and finished climbing:

"Off Belay."

When the belayer hears "off belay" (never sooner) her response ends their communication and their climbing agreement:

"The belay is off."

When a rope is being pulled down from the anchor :

"Rope!"

NOTE
ALWAYS BE ALERT AND AWARE WHEN BELAYING, DOUBLE-CHECK ALL SYSTEMS, AND COMMUNICATE WITH YOUR PARTNER.

Chapter Four

CLIMBING

With all the systems safety checked and in proper order, you are ready to climb. Your climbing gym will have an area or several routes specifically for warming up. Even if you feel you might be able to ascend a steeper or more difficult route, start with something manageable. You will then be able to acquaint yourself with the height, with your body's vertical movement, and with trusting your belayer to catch your fall or lowering. It is a good idea to warm up your muscles and tendons every time you climb, to avoid injury later.

There are many tips and techniques which may be offered to climbers to improve their climbing skill. One approach for the new climber is experiential-experimental. This is suggested because you won't be able to do everything you want (or perhaps are physically capable of) on the first day, or in the first week for that matter. As a new climber you have a clean slate in terms of your notions of what will work and what won't for climbing. This is to your advantage. Try to devote your initial climbing ventures to experiencing and experimenting with movement, balance, and rest without putting big expectations on yourself.

There are dozens of more advanced training approaches and publications which delve into them. Offered here are suggestions and questions to aid you in experimenting with using your feet, movement or weight shift, balance, and rest.

Use Your Feet

Put your weight on them, trust them, and utilize them to save your strength by resting on them. This is the single most important thing you will learn how to do and it is what many experienced climbers have a difficult time incorporating into their vocabulary of moves. Experiment with your ability to stand on virtually nothing, thanks to the sticky rubber on your soles and a little faith. Always look for foot holds as you ascend the wall. Feel stuck? Look for a foot hold, exhale, and move to it.

Bouldering in a gym

Shift Your Weight

Ascending a wall can be reduced to weight shift which, when strung together, can create movement. You start on the ground, and then place each of your hands on a hold. One foot, say the left, stays on the ground while the right finds a hold. You shift your weight onto your right foot, balance, and straighten that leg. You place your left foot on a hold, balance, and straighten your leg. Your hands move up, followed by your feet. Soon you are at the top.

It sounds simple and really it is. Experiment with shifting your weight from foot to foot. Your weight should be entirely on your feet, the muscles of your hands and arms can relax. Try to center your weight on the inside edge of your foot between the big toe and the ball, or the outside edge of your shoe near the little toe. Use your hands to stabilize yourself and only engage your arm muscles when you really need them - it's just like crying wolf: use your arms when you don't need to and they won't be there when you really need them. Your body will create its own flow and rhythm for movement. Avoid forced movements and you'll tend to avoid injuries.

Find a Balance Point

Use balance as part of your weight shift or movement. In movement, balance is like a pause for your body. With it you have a still point, and you create a moment to think and to breathe before shifting your weight and moving to a new position. This is key: all moments of balance may be, slight as it may seem, utilized as a rest position. Developing an ability to seize moments of rest will build your endurance, and generally endurance will carry you farther than strength.

Pumped is the term climbers use for the feeling your forearms often have after climbing. If you are climbing and you find your arms getting really fatigued, find a more efficient body position. Shift your weight to increase your endurance and never hang out too long in one spot, and always continue to *breathe*. To avoid injuries it is best to stop climbing before you are so tired you lose your technique.

Rest

Climbing may sweep you off your feet, but don't let it send you to the doctor. New climbers are incredibly vulnerable to injury, especially injury to the tendons. When climbing, your tendons are utilized in ways uncommon to daily life. Because tendon strength develops much slower than muscle strength, your tendons are exposed to quick damage. Virtually every climber has a sob story about tendonitis. Try to avoid it by warming up thoroughly, stretching, and taking it slow.

Hans Flourine Bouldering

Chapter Five

RATING CLIMBING ROUTES

Your climbing gym will employ some form of rating system for the climbing routes established there. Commonly different routes are marked with different color tape - only the most organized gym managers will insist that all the green-taped routes are of the same rating and all of the blue-taped routes some other rating. Most often, however, whatever color of tape is readily available to the route setter is used. The route setter and other gym employees will then decide the rating of the climb. Route setting is a very subjective practice.

The classification of climbing routes is often confusing to new climbers. Classifications one through six are briefly described, followed by more elaborate explanations of both class five and six climbing. These classifications are generally recognized throughout America, but in almost every country where climbing is popular a different numerical system for rating the difficulty of a route exists.

Class 1:

Essentially walking upright where no special footwear or gear is required qualifies as Class 1 climbing.

Class 2:

Rock scrambling; requires the hiker to occasionally use their hands for assistance. Hiking up a talus slope often is Class 2 climbing.

Class 3:

Class 3 climbing occurs when a slope becomes steep enough to require the hiker to use proper climbing techniques. Having a rope available for beginners to use is advisable.

Class 4:

Exposure is increased in Class 4 climbing, falls resulting in serious injury are possible. Technical knowledge is necessary, and a rope is essential for many climbers.

Class 5:

This class includes the majority of climbing you will find in any gym, and it is the point where many consider rock climbing to begin. Falls from a Class 5 route are often fatal, and use of a rope and other equipment is essential. Hand and foot holds are generally smaller than in Class 4 climbing, but there are ample usable holds to climb the surface without relying on equipment to aid ascent.

Class 6:

In Class 6 climbing, commonly known as *Aid Climbing* or just *Aid*, the climber must rely on proper placement of equipment to ascend the route. Holds and cracks are not large enough or adequate for unaided ascension as in Class 5 climbing. This is the type of climbing many use to ascend Yosemite's *Big Walls*.

The classification of particular routes is generally reserved for fifth and sixth class climbing. Class 5 climbing is divided into grades using a decimal system. The grades range from 5.0 through 5.9. For routes 5.10 and beyond, a letter grade subdivision - a, b, c, or d - is used, "a" being the easiest, increasing in difficulty to "d." Once a "d" grade is reached, the number jumps up one, for example 5.10d becomes 5.11, which is followed by 5.11a, 5.11b, 5.11c, 5.11d, 5.12, 5.12a and so on to the current highest rating. For many years 5.14+, has been the unsurpassable level of difficulty.

The rating of climbing routes is somewhat subjective and open to change. The person who does the first ascent *(puts up the route)*, is in a position to rate it, to assign a numerical and letter grade to it. In America, the rating of a climb generally corresponds to the difficulty of the single hardest move on the route.

In other countries, and increasingly in America on the most difficult of routes, ratings are assigned based on how difficult the climb is as a whole. For example, some routes rated 5.14 may be a string of difficult moves linked together, none of which are actually 5.14 moves. But, because of the difficulty level in linking the moves together, the climb as a whole is considered 5.14. Once others have climbed the same route, they will verify the rating, or suggest the route be *down graded* or *up graded.*

Furthermore, a 5.10 climb in one area may be dramatically different in difficulty from a 5.10 in another area, depending on the local standards. In some areas *sandbagging,* or rating routes less difficult than they really are is popular. It is advisable to know what the local standards are before pushing your limits as a leader.

The difficulty of a climbing route becomes more evident the more one climbs. Subtle differences will become more obvious, especially when one hits a barrier, commonly at the 5.11 or 5.12 level.

In Class 6 or Aid climbing the rating scale is different again. The capital letter "A" is used to represent Class 6 or Aid climbing. A number between one and five is also assigned. Hence Class 6 ratings consist of A1, A2, A3, A4, and A5, A5 being the most difficult. Class 6 routes often take more than one day to complete, requiring climbers to eat and sleep in the vertical realm.

Routes (both Class 5 and Class 6), may be divided into *pitches.* A pitch is essentially one rope length, or whatever the distance between belay points.

Ratings of Aid routes are generally based on the most difficult pitch of the route. Falls in Class 5 climbing may be more frequent than in Class 6 climbing, but consequences of falling on Class 6 routes may be more severe.

Chapter Six

CLIMBERS

Climbers are a diverse group consisting of very individualistic people. Climbers are serious about their fun and those who are good climbers are serious about safety. The bonds made while climbing are significant and never taken lightly. Climbers, while quirky, are generally a good natured, healthy bunch of people though they would deny ever being a group.

Professional Climbers

Professional climbers are an interesting breed. Making a living as a professional climber is a lot more work than just climbing a few hard routes. The climber must be really good, and even then there is promotional work or slide shows to be done for sponsors. Professional climbers don't receive the big purses that other sports enjoy, and there is still inequality between the sexes in terms of prizes at competitions. But sport climbing has come a long way since 1990, and it continues to grow and expand thanks to volunteer efforts by the American Sport Climbers Federation (ASCF).

Hans Florine "Speed"

Hans Florine is the fastest climber in the world. He is a professional sport climber who competes, climbs, and tours North America and Europe on a routine basis. Hans was the 1991 World Champion in speed climbing, and he has competed in over 75 difficulty competitions, winning 17 of them. Hans has been a member of the US climbing team for more than three years, and he is the Executive Director of the American Sport Climbers Federation (ASCF).

His list of achievements runs on to include a BS in Economics, concentrations in Production Operations and Human Resource Management; APICS, CPIM certifications. He received an All American in the pole-vault.

Hans Florine & Kingsley Learner in Yosemite

Hans is as well known for his character and charm as he is for his speed climbing. Hans is *fast*. He has set, broke and holds speed records on the *Nose* and *Salathe* routes on El Capitain in Yosemite National Park 1990, '91, '92, '93. He is one of two humans to solo the *Nose* in a day. During the summer of 1993 he completed a twenty day marathon climbing adventure where twenty classic routes in North America were climbed within twenty days.

Hans discusses speed climbing and the ASCF:

"Speed is power in sport climbing, and speed is safety in the mountains. Speed climbing is probably the most natural way to compare one's climbing prowess. The first climbing competitions ever were speed climbing competitions, often held in what was then the Eastern Block countries. Straight from the actual use of speed in traditional mountaineering, speed translates to safety in the mountains and it is often the only means to a successful ascent. Speed is a natural venue for the first competitions in climbing rather than testing the gymnastic difficulty of climbers.

"I think I have excelled in speed climbing competitions and just plain speed climbing outdoors because of the cross training I have done which includes running, biking, pole-vaulting, swimming, triathalons, and weight training. So few climbers do any physical activity other than climbing. Swimming is probably the greatest single non-climbing activity one can engage in to benefit one's speed climbing.

"When you speed climb you have to give up all that you've learned about 'normal' climbing. You should never look at your feet, if possible. Looking at your feet hinders your upward motion. When on the ground look up at the route and memorize the best hand sequence to use. Go over the sequence as many times as you can in your head.

"Your feet should be 'tread milling' up the wall and your feet should 'remember' where holds are from your hand having just left them. Try to think about 'throwing' the hand holds to the ground. Very important: two, or even three, small or short moves will be faster than one long move. Try to flow up the wall in a continuous motion rather than stopping and lunging and resetting and lunging. Never give up, if you slip, keep going. If the opponent is way ahead, keep cranking. If you're sure you'll lose, keep pulling because you never know how it will turn out.

"When you practice for speed climbing, get on a route well below your ability. This will allow you to flow up it rather than stopping and going. Speed routes should be quite easy in their difficulty level. Try to visualize a fast sequence before getting on the route and 'working it out.' Sometimes speed competitions are on-sight, so it is good to practice that aspect before doing laps on a route over and over again."

No doubt Hans will keep amazing all of us. He continues to climb at competitions when he is not running them. Hans' passion to explore and master the art of light and fast on the rock and in the mountains will surely break more records.

The ASCF

Hans Florine encourages serious climbers to become members of the ASCF. The ASCF is the American organization for competitive sport climbers. As a member of the ASCF, competitors are eligible for points and ranking. Membership dues are paid on a yearly basis. Benefits of becoming a member include newsletters, ranking, competition discounts, and day passes at climbing gyms for members ranked in the top 30. As membership grows, benefits will increase. Requests for applications or information should be directed to:

American Sport Climbers Federation
35 Greenfield Drive
Moraga, CA 94556

Steve Schneider "Crimpers"

Steve Schneider began climbing in 1970 at the age of ten. His father taught him how to climb. Steve liked the movement and the challenge of climbing, finding it much better than basketball or any other sport he had tried. Though his list of achievements is impressive, Steve has "things to do" and they leave him little choice but to keep climbing.

Steve spent eight summers on the Tuolumne Meadows Search and Rescue team in Yosemite National Park. On granite domes with their knobs, glacier polish, and cracks Steve developed his forte: *crimpers.*

Steve Schneider

Project Climb: "How do you define crimper?"

Steve Schneider: "Crimpers are small edges on vertical to slightly overhanging walls. Very hard to climb. I have found the best way to work on this type of hand and foot hold is to develop strength and utilize a reserve technique. Have something saved to kick into when it is needed. Know that the extra strength is there and utilize it. Reducing the weight on arms will aid in the fight of gravity."

PC: "Climbing very technical routes seems to demand foot work, and your foot work is exceptional."

Schneider: "Foot work is critical, and it is something beginning climbers can have a tough time with. Those with enough upper body strength to haul themselves up the wall, without utilizing their feet, can be at a real disadvantage as learning to use your feet may be difficult. The less upper body strength you have, the more inclined to using your feet you may be.

"One thing to think about is turn-out, or the ability for the inside edge of your foot and ankle to be next to the wall and be turned out from the hip so not to damage the knee. Utilizing the inside edge of your foot will get you far on small holds. If you have a big hold, placing your heel on it will allow you to rest by taking the weight off your toes. By spreading your feet out in a stem position you will be able to rest."

PC: "What is your approach for working on a difficult routes?"

Schneider: "Get comfortable with the moves. Do the crux, or hardest part of the route, three times in a row. Repetition right before the climb, then rest. The body will relax yet the muscles will recall enough to do the moves without thinking. I know what needs to be done and my body responds."

PC: "Do you have any tips for getting through a crux?"

Schneider: "Use aimers - chalk marks to direct where your hands or feet should go. They help you to get the hold exactly where and how you want it."

PC: "What advice can you offer to climbers just getting started in the gym?"

Schneider: "Don't climb hard at first. You will injure yourself. Your weak link is between your fingers and elbows. Take time to develop your tendon strength gradually.

"You will probably see a sharp increase in improvement at first, but this will level off as you get better. It eventually becomes a lot harder to get a little better. Don't be discouraged! Climb two days on, one day off and get aerobic every day. Swim, bike, or whatever - get your heart rate up and sweat.

"Steve has climbed every 5.13 in Tuolumne Meadows (he's put up one-third of them). His route *Raging Waters* rated 5.13c on Medlicot Dome is among them. An Eagle Scout, Steve is an adventurer at heart having made the first descent of Lee Vining Canyon in a parapont, kayaked numerous Class 5 rivers, and he is among the leaders of course setting for competitions in America.

"His time of 21 hours and 44 minutes solo on El Capitan's Salathe is impressive. He placed fourth at Snowbird in 1990 and has competed in numerous National and World Cup competitions. Steve's goals for the future are impressive, and no doubt he will see them met."

Caroline Peck "Boundless"

Caroline Peck was born in Scotland in 1955. She has traveled the world learning a variety of professions. She is a chiropractor, a Shiatsu therapist, a student acupuncturist, a teacher and a farmer. She began climbing in October of 1993. With boundless energy and a limitless imagination for what is possible, Caroline is climbing well and continues to learn about herself through the sport.

Caroline Peck

"A few years back I went to Yosemite Valley. I knew nothing about climbing, I had never even seen a climbing harness. There was a moment though when I was facing a huge granite wall. At that point I knew I would climb. Seeing the wall made my body recall a feeling for movement it has always known. I have participated in every sport possible, and one day on the tennis courts my friend Grace told me about the new climbing gym in town; there was a women's course starting soon. I asked about the teacher: 'was she a good climber?' Grace told me she was ranked tenth in the nation. That night I called and signed up for the course.

"When I first got on the climbing wall, my body seemed to know what to do, it was like I had been doing it all my life. The movement was really enjoyable. There are several things I think climbing can do for anyone.

"Climbing will make your body strong. It is a symmetrical strength which develops without thinking about it. One just needs to climb and the muscles naturally become strong and *useful*. Climbing is different than weight training in that sense. Both will make you strong, but through climbing you utilize your strength. The incentive to climb is climbing.

"Climbing in the gym will prepare you physically for climbing outdoors. I don't think I would have climbed as well as I did outside had I not started in a gym. I had never been scared of climbing until I went outside. In the gym I was able to enjoy the movement aspects of climbing without the environmental factors present on real rock.

"Climbing brought me back to my childhood. I feel like a kid playing in adult clothing. While climbing you can do things without thinking 'this is too hard.' Adults create many barriers and control them carefully. Climbing in the gym allows one to lose control and still be safe. You get to choose a degree of challenge and test yourself without risking physical safety.

"No one can climb a route for me and no one can tell me how to climb. I may be fluid one day and clumsy the next, but whatever I do, it is entirely mine. I achieve something every time I climb. I may climb something I never tried before, discover a new way to use my feet or get one hold higher on a route I have been trying for days. Whatever the case, improvement is notable, and there is a lot of fulfillment for your investment.

"The more I climb the more alive I feel. I think that life must be exciting and lived with a bit of fear. We all seek excitement in one sense or another, be it physical, emotional, or intellectual. Climbing brings the three together. It is challenging to the body, spirit, and mind in a way no other activity is. Climbing reveals the limits of my mind and through it I am able to transcend those barriers. I have been able to find, test, and redefine my limits because you must be totally present to climb effectively - even if it is on a route which is easy for you. The days you can't climb are the days you aren't there.

"Climbing opens up the world of the body and what it is capable of doing. It is a whole new way of finding yourself. Climbing offers an opportunity for people of all levels of fitness and all abilities to feel their bodies in a new way. No matter how good of a climber one becomes, one must always be present to climb. Climbing demands that you find that place of 'now' or 'still.' You have to be there no matter what. Everyone should try climbing a wall at least once in their lives, even if you are afraid of heights or feel you are not strong enough to do it. You'll never know what climbing will reveal to you until you try it!"

Doug Englekirk "Endurance"

Doug Englekirk started climbing in 1981 at the age of twenty. He had always loved the outdoors, and the thrill and adventure of climbing met this love with passion. His list of personal bests includes a solo ascent of the "Nose" route on El Capitain in 24 /12 hours and the first ascent of the route Genesis also on the big stone, El Capitain. In 1992 and 1993 he won the National Sport Climbing Championships. A conversation with him in isolation at the 1994 Sport Climbing Nationals held at City Rock in June reveals his love for climbing and his strengths:

Project Climb: "You seem to excel at both climbing on rock and climbing indoors, especially in competition. What are the advantages of indoor climbing?"

Doug Englekirk: "It can be like climbing on real rock, but it's greatest advantage for me is the controlled training environment which allows me to improve on real rock."

PC: "What is your forte and why is that your strength?"

DE: "Tenacity and endurance tend to be what allows me to succeed in difficult situations. In climbing it keeps me from giving up until I have nothing left. In life I tend to be a hard worker (Doug is a contractor) which my clients like. Another strength in climbing which helps perhaps more is not my strength, but that which strengthens me. It is the peace of God which surpasses all understanding. My relationship with Christ gives me the peace I need to endure. I know God is in control, no matter what happens. This allows me to not let stressful situations get to me - but my trust is not always complete, so I'm far from stress-free. My faith helps me in a competition setting. For example, I need not fret about who's competing or the conditions because God is on my side. His perfect will may be for me to win or to lose and that is for my eventual good and His glory.

PC: "What is your involvement with Solid Rock, Climbers for Christ?"

DE: "I am not at the core of that organization, but I speak to the group and support what they are doing."

PC: "What advice would you offer someone who is just starting out, especially in terms of climbing inside?"

DE: "Where do I begin? First, climb because you enjoy it. Learn your skills well - harness, knots, belaying, communication, anchors when you go outside. Don't expect climbing outside to be like climbing indoors. A lot is involved when climbing outdoors; it is a serious endeavor and should be approached with respect and knowledge. Warm up thoroughly and always have fun."

Wayne Willoughby "Adversity & Perseverance"

Wayne Willoughby is an accomplished rock climber and alpinist. His ascents are numerous and noteworthy. He is like other climbers in his passion for climbing and a mile long list of routes he wants to ascend. Two things set him apart from other climbers: he is more action than talk and he is disabled.

Born in 1952, Wayne contracted the polio virus as an infant. He had his first surgery at two. While spending months at a time motionless in a full-body cast, he had time to reflect on the world. As a result, Wayne knew that life would take him in interesting directions. Between operations as a kid, Wayne was able to play Little

League baseball, swim, and surf. At twelve he was back for more orthopedic surgery. One procedure was botched, and at nineteen, two inches of bone were removed from his right femur and a metal rod was inserted through his hip to correct the mistake. This leg operation left him unable to surf.

Wayne Willoughby

His determination to pursue his passion for sports, bicycling and motorcycles filled some of the void left by his inability to surf. While in college, Wayne picked up basketball, swimming competitively and he played on the water polo team. Wayne also began making frequent trips to Yosemite to climb towering granite walls.

The world seemed determined to toss difficult blows Wayne's way: he was struck by a car on his motorcycle leaving his left knee torn apart. Another incident brought on Post Polio Syndrome resulting in significant health problems and atrophy throughout his body.

Over the next five years Wayne endured countless hours of physical therapy, rehabilitating himself enough to play both basketball and water polo successfully again. Encouraged by his progress, Wayne and his climbing partner made a successful ascent of the Zodiac route on El Capitan in Yosemite Valley. This ascent was significant both physically and symbolically for Wayne; it carried him through the winter season with hope for more climbing.

In the spring of 1991, Wayne and his partner were making plans to climb Half Dome in Yosemite Valley when he was brutally assaulted and left with injuries to his knee, ankle and back. With a lot of physical therapy and even more faith, Wayne brought his body back to health. His plans to continue climbing never waivered.

On August 5, 1994, Wayne and his partners Mike O'Donnell and Bill Witt, along with members of the Thrillseekers Climbing Gym in Denver, CO, set out on their next adventure: the DI - up the Diamond on Longs Peak. Wayne was carried three of the five-mile approach to the route. This 14,255' granite mountain in the heart of the Rockies has proven to be a challenge to climbers of all abilities. Mike, Bill and Wayne had been planning this trip for two years. An accomplished climber, Mike had lost a climbing partner and several toes on this mountain. He kept up the pace for both Bill and Wayne.

The conditions were harsh. The night was spent at the base of the mountain sleeping restlessly. Wayne felt blessed to be in such an amazing environment of towering rock, snow and ice. To be there with his companions was a powerful experience; how could one express this feeling effectively to others when asked, "Why do you climb?"

Eight pitches were climbed on the first day; the going was slow and consistently difficult. By the end of the day, the climbers achored cots into the granite wall more than a thousand feet from the ground. After dinner, Wayne's partners passed out, exhausted from the day's work. Wayne could hardly sleep. He was excited by the environment and spectacular perspective.

The sun warmed the climbing partners as they continued their ascent the next morning. Mike led the first pitch which Wayne followed, removing the wired nuts and "friends" Mike used as anchor points of protection. The weather was a ubiquitous issue to contend with on Long's Peak. The team encountered a storm moving in. The wind picked up and they knew it would slow their progress if not shut them down completely. Climbing well into the night through the icey wind, and suffering muscle spasms throughout, Wayne and his partners reached the top and spent a chilly night on the mountain before completing their descent in the morning.

The ascent of this route is notable for any climber. Wayne Willoughby not only accomplished his goal of making the ascent, he once again conquered the many disabling odds against him. He is a role model for many physically challenged individuals and an inspiration to us all.

Barry Bates "Feet"

Born in 1949, Barry Bates has been climbing for more than 30 years. His climbing style is revealed in his calm, deliberate demeanor. Barry is meticulous about his foot work, placing his feet on holds with intention and integrity. Barry has seen climbing evolve from an activity for the wild and recluse during the early sixties, to a sport for families and others who might be identified as part of the mainstream. Barry began his climbing endeavors with his father, an artist and poet, in Monterey County, California. By 1964, young Barry turned his sights on climbing the towering walls of Yosemite Valley.

Barry Bates

"The first climbing I did in the Valley included Washington's Column and Arrowhead Spire. Climbing was really an extension of backpacking then. There was no one to teach us what to do, so we just learned as we went along. Some of the scariest experiences I have ever had while climbing were on easier routes run-out 40 to 50 feet. We didn't have the type of protection or equipment available today, and off-width cracks just couldn't be protected with pitons."

In 1968, Barry was 19 years old and 5.10 was considered the hardest climbing around. Routes which were difficult then - Twilight Zone, Chingando, Vendetta and Crack of Doom - still prove to be challenging to climbers today. Barry was getting up those routes and a few years later he was doing the first ascents of classics such as Lunatic Fringe, Five and Dime, and New Dimensions.

"There was no 'cutting edge' back then. We were just people who liked to climb - Jim Bridwell, Kim Schmitz, Phil Gleason, Steve Wunsch, the late Bev Johnson, and others. We were interested in pushing our limits and having fun too."

Barry's incredible strength was developed slowly through years of bouldering.

"Bouldering filled a void back then which sport climbing fulfills now. When we were out leading something, it usually wasn't gymnastically the most difficult climbing we were able to do. We could work out difficult gymnastic problems on the boulders around Camp 4 to increase our skill for doing first ascents. Today first ascents are more artistic in the sense that the bolts should be placed to create the best possible routes. Sport areas are really outdoor recreation facilities, so why not make them as safe and fun as possible?"

At 22, Barry started college at San Jose State University as an art and history student. He earned an MA in art, focusing on ceramic sculpture. Barry continued to climb and earn his living as an artist for several years. He met and married Debbie, a sociologist who he met through climbing. Together they moved to Alaska where they lived for five years. Prior to the birth of their first child, they returned to the Santa Cruz area.

Barry didn't climb seriously between 1980 and 1989, but he realized that at 40 he was becoming "soft." Not wanting to follow in Elvis' footsteps of weight gain and demise, Barry began climbing seriously again. At 45, Barry is a climbing machine: fitness, strength, endurance, experience and talent mixed in with a dry sense of humor.

Barry's comments on climbing indoors: "I like climbing indoors because I never get scared and I can climb more with my kids."

Regarding his indoor climbing and his own ability: "I have learned to follow the colored tape routes, but I can't climb like the 12-year-olds there."

Andres Puhvel "Fun"

Andres Puhvel first tried climbing at the age of 14 because he thought it would be fun. He was right. With a love for the outdoors and adventure, Andy embraced climbing. By the time he was 15 he had climbed Half Dome, and by 17 he was setting speed records in Yosemite. Andres is motivated by a healthy sense of fun, taking delight in all his endeavors.

Andres Puhvel

"[My climbing friends and I] tried to set speed records because it seemed like a fun challenge. Why not? We had the ability and the confidence to do it, and because of this we were able to take climbing lightly. I think it comes down to the fact that you must make your own decisions about safety - nothing is written in stone - but you should also be prepared to accept the consequences of poor judgment. My confidence is based in experience and a clear understanding of the line which separates real risk from perceived risk."

Andy appeared in *Details* magazine several years ago:

"All 6'6" 150 pounds of me - it was a side bar about a competition and the foul words which flowed out of my mouth when I fell off the speed route."

Without apology, Andy attributes his frustration to his age, 17, at the time. During college Andy spent time performing as a circus climber in Germany, "We dressed up like Evel Kneviel and paraded around in front of 400 German tourists."

Andy graduated from UC Santa Cruz with a degree in Russian History. Though he continues to climb well and retains the speed record on the Salathe of 8 hours and 56 minutes, he considers himself neither an historian nor a climber. When asked what he does he says, "Nothing. Absolutely nothing." Drive by his seedy apartment on Mission Street (it's above a bar) any night, at two or three in the morning, and you'll see Andy at his best. Andy is hunched over, illuminated by a bare light bulb. The Bee Gee's are blasting through his walkman. He works on his laboriously detailed creations intensely into the wee hours of the morning. He rises early only to Rollerblade to the climbing gym to work with at-risk students as a Project Climb director. Of his job as a Pacific Edge instructor and route setter, "If you have to make money you might as well have fun doing it."

Martha Robrahn "Functional Mobility"

Martha Robrahn is a former computer engineer who now practices body work to help people enhance the quality of their lives. As she puts it, "I used to do systems analysis on computers. I now do it with people and it's a lot more fun!"

Martha Robrahn

Martha enjoys climbing because she meets such wonderful people and it gives her a chance to develop her body in ways bicycling, hiking, cross country skiing and yoga do not. Through climbing, Martha has learned to work effectively with climbers to help them feel more relaxed and climb better. She has written the following section based on a series of movements she selected and adapted specifically for climbers to increase their functional mobility.

Becoming Functionally Mobile

Climbing requires both strength and flexibility which must be applied *in motion* (and often at odd angles) to be useful for climbing. This is *functional mobility*. The Trager® Approach to movement education is utilized in the following to assist you in improving your climbing by enhancing your functional mobility. Rather than building muscle, the goal of Trager is to use simple movements to maintain and enhance the mobility and functionality of the muscles you already have.

Trager Psychophysical Integration (a unique form of body work) and Mentastics® Movement Education are the discovery of Milton Trager, MD ("Trager" and "Mentastics" are registered service marks of the Trager Institute). Trager first began developing this approach as a teenager when he was an amateur gymnast and boxer. For the next 50 years he refined and expanded his discovery. Trager work is now helping people live better in their bodies in a variety of ways. In addition to helping the average person release the stresses of daily life, Trager work is also used in elite athlete training programs and in enhancing functionality for individuals with neuromuscular disabilities.

Trager may be utilized as a warm-up or cool-down for climbing. The general approach with each movement pattern is the same. Try the movement a couple of times. Notice if the motion is restricted in any way. If so, you may want to make the movement smaller initially until your body releases some of its tension. Now repeat the movement a few times focusing on making the pattern as *smooth* and *effortless* as possible. As your body feels what it is like to move freely, it releases the old tensions and restrictions from disuse or overuse. Mobility increases and a deeper sense of relaxation results.

• Check-in

Begin in a comfortable standing position and check-in with your body. Notice how you are distributing the weight on your feet (more forward, backward, to the side?). Notice which areas of your body are holding tension (legs, lower back, arms, shoulders, neck, jaw?). Are your shoulders centered above your hips or is there a lean to your body? The first step in the process is to increase your awareness of your body.

• Shifting weight and increasing balance.

A significant portion of our kinesthetic awareness of balance comes from the proprioceptive sensitivity in our feet. This movement pattern is focused on waking up these sensory systems and deepening your awareness of balance. Though we are doing these movements on the ground, the awareness should easily transfer to climbing. Paying attention to your body's signals will help you to realize when a move puts you too far off balance and give you a greater sense of confidence in making transitions that are within your abilities.

Starting from a comfortable standing position, slowly begin to shift the weight on your feet from side to side. Notice when the leg muscles tend to grab to prevent you from falling sideways. Shift your weight within your comfortable range of motion. Experiment with a slightly wider or narrower stance. Try shifting forward and backward. Are there different muscle safety systems engaged to prevent your falling backwards and forwards? Since climbing often requires an open stance, turn your feet outwards and begin shifting weight again. Get a good sense of the limits of your balance and how your body reacts when you've gone too far. This movement pattern is a great one to practice whenever you are stuck standing in line. The grocery store line is my favorite place.

Once you have become familiar with the basic feeling of shifting weight, you are ready to add the enhancement for climbing - shifting weight *up*. Find a stairway or sturdy surface you can step up onto. With your feet parallel or turned out, slowly begin to shift your weight from the ground to the step and back. Can your take offs and transitions be smooth and effortless? Can your landings be soft? Try higher or wider transitions as your body enhances its abilities.

• Opening the shoulders

Climbers tend to be always reaching forward, sometimes leading to an over development of the upper back, and shoulders that curve forward. This movement pattern is focused on keeping the full range of motion open in the shoulder girdle.

With your right hand, scribe an arc from the left side of your head, over your head, out to the far right, and ending by dropping behind your back. Remembering to stay within your comfortable range of motion, do a few of these with your right arm. Now pause and compare the left and right shoulders. Is the right a bit further back? Does it have a more relaxed quality? Good, you're getting the idea. Now balance out by opening the left side.

• Arm & leg shimmers

Climbing really challenges our arm and leg muscles to be strong and flexible at the same time. Over tight muscles can lead to stress and strain injuries that can take a long time to heal. These movements are designed to make sure that your muscles have that little extra slack so they can be put to the test in unusual ways.

Begin in a comfortable standing position. Lean over to the right and allow your right arm to hang easily from your shoulder. Now begin to create a clockwise and counter clockwise partial rotation of your arm (a bit like strumming a guitar).

Find a rhythm and speed that create a shimmering or rippling effect in your upper arm muscles. Get a sense of the muscles being able to rotate slightly around the bones. As this occurs, the muscles relax, allowing you to make that extra long reach or dyno for a hold. Is there a different rhythm that will shimmer your forearm? Now check the feeling quality between your left and right arms. Is the right arm a little softer? Is the elbow a bit straighter? Does the arm hang a little lower? Great! Now shimmer out the left arm in a similar manner.

Now apply a similar approach to the leg muscles. Stand on your right leg and move your left leg to the side slightly, keeping your toes on the ground for stability. Set up a rotational back and forth movement in your left leg that creates that sense of the muscles rotating slightly around the bones. The rhythm may be different for your calves than for your thighs. Can the ripples of your muscles over the bones be as fluid as water flowing down a stream? Pause and feel the difference in your legs. Now repeat the process for your right leg.

• Pelvic rocks

Our lower backs often take a lot of strain in our daily lives. This movement pattern is designed to relax and open the mobility of the lumbar region so it will not limit your climbing.

Begin by lying on your back with your knees bent so that your feet can be flat on the floor. Focusing on the very front of your hips, see how far towards your head and feet that these bones can comfortably move. Now see if you can set up an up (towards your head) and down (towards your feet) movement in your hips by pushing your body up slightly (towards your head) with your feet and then letting it rebound back towards your feet. This should set up rocking motion in your pelvis and low back that will gradually release tension in the low back. It's not important here to move your pelvis through its full range of motion. Focus instead on making the motion smooth and springy.

• Opening the hips

Getting really close to the wall when climbing requires flexibility from our pelvis and legs. This movement pattern focuses on opening the mobility of the hips and the lateral flexibility of the thigh muscles.

Begin by lying on your back with your knees bent so that your feet can be flat on the floor. Now drop both legs to the left side. Slowly begin to move your right knee up and over towards the right side, keeping your knees bent and feet in contact with the floor. For most people, the restriction in the inner thigh area will require you to follow the right leg with the left eventually. This is to be expected. As your right leg goes past vertical, allow gravity to take over and let the leg drop softly to the floor. Follow with the left leg dropping softly on the right. Now reverse the process, moving the legs back to the left side. Repeat a few times to make the process fluid.

• Releasing the neck

Climbers spend a lot of their time looking up, either for the next hold or watching their partners on belay. This tends to create neck tension particularly at the base of the skull in the suboccipital area. This pattern will help you release the tensions in your neck.

Do you know what an infinity sign is? It looks like a sideways figure 8 (∞). Begin to draw infinity signs in the air with your nose. Small patterns will release the tension at the base of your skull. Larger patterns will address more general neck tension. Remember to make the movements smooth. After you have done a few of these, stop and go the other direction with the pattern. (If you were moving down from the center, go up instead or vice versa.) Often, one direction will be easier than the other. Practice both.

You can apply this movement pattern almost anywhere: when you're belaying your partner, when you're stopped at a signal while driving, while you're watching TV or listening to music. Get in the habit of making these movements an integral part of your daily routine.

• Invent your own

Each of us has unique areas of our bodies that carry extra tension and stress. You can make up your own movements to help these places relax by applying the principles we have learned in these movement patterns. First, notice where the tension or restriction is. Next, find a movement pattern that creates mobility in the affected muscle groups. Now find a way to do this movement with ease, fluidity, and, if possible, without using the muscles you are trying to relax. Applying the principles of momentum and gravity are often useful here.

Climbers tend to carry tension in their fingers. Your assignment is to create a movement pattern that allows you to release the tension in your fingers. It might be a modification of the arm shimmers or perhaps a way of flicking your wrist that gives your fingers that chance to open their mobility and relax their muscles again. Did you find one? Great!

• Check-in

Again, pause and check in with your body. How do you feel? More relaxed? Lighter? More balanced? How has the overall tension level in your body changed? Give yourself a chance to really absorb the feeling. Now go and try climbing with this new sense of your body and when you notice that sense of ease lessening, remember to take a break!

• Take a break!

Sometimes, in mid-ascent, your body will be telling you that it needs a break: your fingers are cramping, a leg begins to shake (known as "sewing machine leg"), your arms or shoulders feel fatigued. It is often possible to pause for a moment in the middle of a climb and apply some of the self care movements we have discussed.

If you have two good footholds and a handhold, take the opportunity to open the shoulder girdle, shimmer the arm muscles and loosen the fingers. An upright version of the pelvic rock can help to ease out low back tension. With two handholds and a foothold, you can shimmer the tension from a leg.

If you have time to chalk, you probably also have time to take care of your body. If you get in the habit of paying attention and releasing the tension while you climb, you are much less likely to over stress your muscles and tendons. Additionally, you will probably be able to climb for longer periods of time.

• Injury prevention

No matter how careful we are with our bodies, sooner or later we will tend to over stress them. When this happens, it is important to take care of yourself. Take a few days off to allow your body to rest and heal. Find a good body work practitioner in your area and treat yourself to a session. A small break now can help to prevent long term problems.

• Happy ascents to you

I hope this section has given you some new tools for enhancing your functional mobility, your body awareness, and your climbing pleasure.

The Trager Approach is taught through the Trager Institute (33 Millwood, Mill Valley, CA 94941, 415/388-2688). Contact the Institute for more information on The Trager Approach or for a referral to a certified practitioner in your area.

Erika Atkins "Strength"

Erika Atkins is a fine artist focused on oil painting. She graduated from Yale University in 1991. Painting is her life's love and work and climbing is an activity she engages in several times a week. She has been climbing since 1991.

"I recommend climbing to *all* women. I find it empowering. To look at a rock and know you can climb at least some of it is colossal. It is wonderful to know that I can make my body move, that I can make the next reach, that I have the strength to continue. I think far too many women (in the US anyway) are socialized to dislike, even despise our bodies, to betray our physical abilities, to refuse strength in an attempt to be "feminine." Climbing has helped me reject that teaching and is allowing me to acknowledge my *whole* self as big, strong, beautiful.

Erika Atkins

"New climbers should take it slow. Be easy with yourself. Get some tips from experienced climbers - it really helps. And always climb both indoors at the gym and out in the 'real world' if possible. Never put yourself in a situation of risk because of carelessness or inexperience. Expect your safety skills to develop slowly and thoroughly. Try to climb as much as you can and it won't hurt to become close friends with a massage therapist! Indoor climbing is more than just 'connect the dots' as it might appear; it is challenging and physically very much like climbing on rock."

Kelly Robbins "Grace"

Kelly Robbins is a sixteen-year old full time student at a Junior College and a part-time sales women in a department store. She was first attracted to climbing when she saw a climbing magazine at a book shop.

"Climbing was the most beautiful athletic activity I had ever seen. I have practiced yoga and modern dance, but these are done in studios or at best on a lawn or at the beach. I also run for endurance, yet climbing tugged at me like no other sport. I started climbing about a year ago and I just love it.

"Every time I am about to begin climbing a route, I imagine that the walls of the gym have fallen away and I am outside climbing on real rock. I love that feeling of freedom and of the movements up a wall. Though I am a beginner, I feel that it is safe to say if you are looking for a sport which blends the mind, body and spirit, take up climbing."

Diane Russell "Competitions"

Diane Russell began technical rock climbing in Colorado when she was just 14 years old. Since then she has dabbled in many forms of climbing: rock, snow and ice, but tends to prefer and excel at rock climbing.

Diane guided six years for the Colorado Mountain School and has taught hundreds of clients safety skills and climbing technique. Guiding and climbing have taken her around the world from New Zealand to the Himalayas, to Europe and all over the United States. Diane is a strong competitive climber having competed in countless National and many World Cup competitions.

Diane is among the top female rock climbers in the nation. Her achievements on stone and in competition are notable. Her quiet direct approach to life is the same attitude she assumes for competition. Diane encourages anyone interested to try competing. Her best competitor tip is: "Climb for yourself and compete as a challenge to yourself, but above all, have fun doing it."

Diane Russell

Women: Climbing For the First Time

A group of women in their twenties tried indoor climbing for the first time with experienced Project Climb students assisting in instruction. The best way to let you know what the new climbers experienced is to let their words be read. Here's what they had to say:

"One of the hardest things I did today was charging up the 5.7 wall and finding myself stuck halfway up. I couldn't figure out what my next move needed to be. Everything seemed physically impossible at that point and I was *so frustrated!* It took me 15 minutes to get past that one rock. It was so friggin' hard, but I was so glad I didn't give up!

"I surprised myself by having an amazing time climbing the walls. Climbing wasn't something I have ever really given thought to doing before. Maybe I thought that I couldn't pull it off - I was surprised at how much I enjoyed myself!

"The thing I loved about today was being with a group of women doing something new to all of us together. I loved climbing that wall all by myself, yet not being alone at it because my friends were at the bottom supporting me all the way. That point of utter frustration was almost too much. I was so angry and physically exhausted. My hand was all scraped up and bleeding, but I kept with it. I loved working past that frustration. I got a high from being with that power. I was working with my body in a way I never have. I feel like we developed a new relationship. I learned I need to trust my body more. I didn't realize my own strength before. I would climb again to try different walls because all the paths up are different. It felt like a puzzle to solve with your body.

"I have been telling my friends to try it for the sake of doing something different and because it was damn fun. I saw my friends and myself face our fear of heights, our fear of quitting and of failure. This experience has given me a sense of worth...in the physical sense of 'I can do things with my body,' and that I am a strong woman regardless of the messages society gives me. Climbing is such a metaphor for life...it showed me that with commitment and perseverance we can do *anything!" Laurel Elizabeth*

"I climbed the 5.5 wall, getting up on it in the first place was really tough. I had to try about ten times to even make the second step. I almost gave up, but I stuck with it and made it to the top!

"I really liked being with my friends, encouraging each other, and making it to the top when I never thought I could. Learning something new - especially something athletic (since I am not what you would call an athlete!) was great. I would love to try climbing again because it was fun, challenging and a great work out. You don't have to be a big sports person to enjoy climbing, it seems like anyone could climb. You can start out on an easier climb and work up to harder ones.

"I loved this experience though it's something I never would have done if Laurel hadn't talked me into it. I worked hard at climbing, but it wasn't impossible and succeeding at climbing, tying the knots and belaying made it so much fun." *Drama Rose*

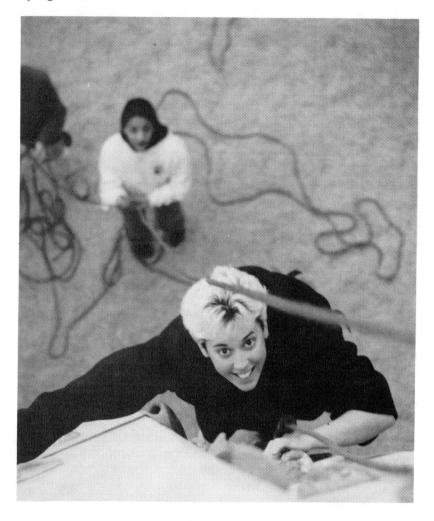

Drama Rose

"It was really hard for me to trust people in terms of their climbing skills. Since I managed to get out of bed to keep this commitment, I decided to go for it anyway. I felt like I wasn't ready to really challenge myself with the climbing - I stuck with climbs that I knew I

Climbing is a wonderful thing to do to dispel fear. We walked into Pacific Edge as six individuals and emerged as one cohesive unit - a truly valuable experience." *Ilene Stern*

"The hardest thing I did was also the most powerful thing. I was almost to the top and all I wanted was to touch the last rock. I was three moves away. Those three moves were the hardest. I felt like I was going to bust at the seams when I finally grabbed the last hold!

"I surprised myself the whole time I was there: at putting on the equipment, by not giving up, at my strength and endurance. I loved it when my friends and acquaintances supported me on my journey up that wall, they were with me all the way - that was beautiful! The only time I was really afraid was when I was told it was okay if I wanted to get down when I was frustrated half way through. I was afraid I might, but I didn't!

"In my life I have been known to be many unendearing things, and a quitter is one of those things. This experience was a powerful tool to reinstate some of the faith I have in myself. I had lots of support from people who were telling me that *any* amount of effort, energy, and presence for this activity was going to be respected. This really helped me to drive on and not to quit because I knew that anything I did would be an accomplishment." *Janet Harvie*

"I felt unsure that I could belay Anne Marie - belaying is a big responsibility! I kept climbing even though I was scared. I felt really proud of myself and glad that I pushed my limits. I was surprised at how easily I built trust in my belayers and how I could talk myself through panic moments. When I was stuck for so long, unable to find a path to get higher, I was thinking 'this is impossible, I can't, I can't!' Then I heard what I was telling myself, and I said Shan, you *can*. In a minute you'll be above this place and you will be working on a new problem. And then I reached the rock I needed, found the strength to pull myself up, and was at a new place. My next move was to fall off from fatigue, but that was okay because I loved the whole process. I love that I believed in my ability to persevere.

"Being with women and climbing was wonderful, and having the young women teach us was incredible. They were really great because they were patient and coached us at belaying and climbing. Climbing got me in touch with my brave self, and I felt like a kid playing." *E. Shannon Stavinoha*

Kids As Climbers

Kids are natural climbers, and they seem to thrive in the atmosphere of indoor climbing facilities. The climbing gym is accessible, whereas most climbing areas are not easily accessible to young people. Climbing gyms are a healthy environment for kids of all ages where positive and supportive adult role models are often abundant. The underlying motivation for all these climbers seems to be fun.

Kolya Noble and Nisse Noble

Sisters Kolya (Koko) and Nisse Noble were introduced to climbing on a school field trip to Pacific Edge. They had never climbed indoors before, but instantly fell in love with it. Their mother, Gayle, the Senior Design Engineer at Quantum, a computer firm in the Silicon Valley, is 100% behind their climbing.

Koko, 13, likes the physical part of climbing:

"I like how hard it is. There are always big stretches and small rocks to hold on to. The environment can be challenging too - there are so many cute boys to look at!

"I think it is really cool to be trusted to belay. I am mature enough to do it, but it can be hard. Belaying is a big responsibility and all my focus and attention is on the climber and what I am doing. The feeling that I can set up the safety systems properly makes me feel capable.

"I like being able to work out mentally the problems of ascending the wall. That I can learn to do something I couldn't before is really great. Sometimes it takes a while to figure out a problem and that can be frustrating, but working it out is exciting. I can get excited, nervous and scared all at once when climbing. When I do a challenging climb I feel really good about myself. And there is always something more challenging to do!"

Nisse, 7, is as cute and elfin as her name implies. Her favorite part of climbing is:

"Swinging in the air. I like feeling relaxed high off the ground, it's fun. Going over the top of a wall is really fun too. I feel tired and relieved to get to the ledge, and it is always a little scary coming down.

Nisse Noble

"When I get to the top I can look out the window at the sea, it is so pretty from up high.

"Sometimes it is challenging to grab at a rock and not to get it because it is ungrabable and that can be frustrating. When I can finally figure out a way to do something I couldn't do before I really feel proud. I look forward to doing new things every time I come to the climbing gym."

Gayle has a family membership which includes herself, her two daughters, a son, and extended family members. She enjoys climbing with her kids several times a week. Gayle says this about the benefits of climbing to her family:

"Climbing is a positive way of taking the edge off of living closely with a lot of people. Kids need an outlet for their abundant energy, preferably in a constructive, valuable place. Climbing at the gym has become that for us. My girls, especially Koko, are more responsible and receptive. We all get along better at home. The caliber of people we have met climbing seem educated and are very friendly, a great family atmosphere where you don't have to worry much about who you meet. My kids all have been able to focus more and have really blossomed into confidence since we started climbing."

Adam Long

Adam Long, 12, enjoys the risk, the challenges and the fitness which climbing has offered him. He says this:

"[I like to] push myself beyond my fears, especially when lead climbing. When I am able to do something I thought I couldn't, my confidence is boosted. The physical difficulty of pulling myself up on little tiny rocks is great. I am motivated to do it just to see if it is possible. Climbing has made me a lot stronger and I feel healthier than when I was just mountain biking.

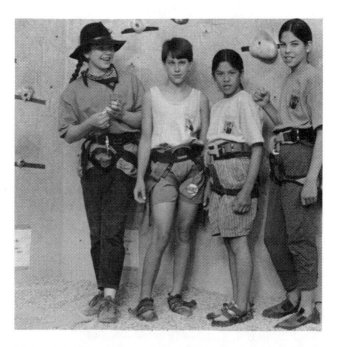

Koko Noble, Adam Long, Jay & Jacob Weber

"Belaying was difficult at first, but it is possible to learn. There is a feeling of being responsible for another person; what *I* do directly affects another person. I never had that much responsibility before.

"Climbing has helped me to have a lot more confidence in myself and in other things like school or when I am in difficult situations. I feel like I can do things I couldn't before. I like having the confidence because I feel like more of a person. Climbing is a big mental, muscle, and endurance builder and it is still fun!"

Jay Weber and Jacob Weber

Jay and Jacob Weber are an amazing pair of kids, and they are also brothers. Jay, 12, explains why he likes climbing:

"It's fun! Getting high off the ground is great. I like bouldering in the cave because doing the movements can be really difficult. Leading is really great too. It can be fun to fall, but it can be a bit scary. Reaching for holds in tough moves and getting them makes me feel I can do things I once thought were impossible.

"It is nice that people trust you to belay them. Only once before when my mom let me swim across the Trinity River did I feel that trusted. I also have to trust my brother to belay me. I never trusted him like that before. We get along better now because we have to.

"I feel really proud of myself when I do hard routes. I have a feeling of accomplishment that I haven't had before. I'm looking forward to climbing outside and to climbing more."

Jacob, 10, feels he's:

"[a] pretty good belayer. I feel good about the responsibility of having someone's life in my hands. I have the skill and the confidence to belay the right way and not hurt anyone.

"Climbing is really fun. It is challenging and makes me think about how to move so I can get up the wall. Sometimes climbing can be scary, like when you're holding on to a little tiny hold and you feel like you'll slip off. Scary makes it exciting and fun too. It doesn't matter if you get to the top as long as you have fun all the way up."

Jay & Jacob Weber

Chris Sharma

Chris Sharma, 13, has excelled at climbing partially because of his openness and willingness to listen and work with others, and by his own intense determination to keep moving. He placed second in his division at the 1994 Junior National Climbing Championships held in Pittsburgh, PA.

Of climbing, Chris likes the aspects of utilizing his "brain and physical power." Chris says:

"It is mentally and physically challenging. It is always fun and never boring. There is always something harder or different to do. There are so many types of climbing. Going outside of the gym opens up all sorts of new things. There are different types of climbing for different types of rocks. Outside you don't have to think about which holds are on or off.

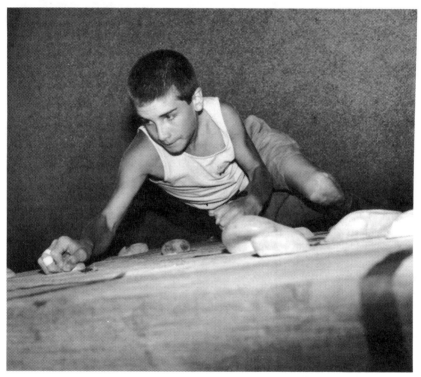

Chris Sharma

"Belaying is a good thing. I don't really think soloing without a rope is a good idea. Belaying can be a good trust builder; if I can trust someone with my life, I can trust them to help me in other ways. People you climb with make really good friends because of the intensity of the experience.

"Sometimes climbing helps me get along better with my dad. I climb with him and he can trust me better because I belay him and he belays me. It was funny to see him climb the first time, but belaying him was no problem.

"Competing is fun because I have gotten to meet other climbers my age and some of the really good older climbers. I can compare my experiences with them and I have made a lot of friends from other states. Traveling is fun too. The pressure of competition helps me climb better and pushes me to do well. I like being in isolation with the other climbers before it is my turn to climb - it is neat to see what their habits are and how they warm up and to learn what kind of people they are.

"Climbing makes me feel good about myself because it is a neat sport. It is good for all kinds of people. Try your hardest and don't worry about points or how high you get. Never be too serious (except with safety) and always have fun with climbing."

Kingsley Lerner

Kingsley Lerner began climbing in 1990 at the age of nine. She was introduced to the sport by her mother, Melanie Lerner. Melanie retains tragic memories of her sister, Carla, who as an adult fell to her death from a cliff. She decided to address her fears at City Rock, one of the earliest climbing gyms in the country, located in Emeryville, CA. Melanie found she was able to conquer her fears and she discovered a challenging and exciting new sport. She eagerly shared her new love with her children Miles and Kingsley.

Kingsley loves climbing because when she is doing it she doesn't have to think about anything else. She likes being able to focus all her attention on one thing, then accomplishing her goal. Kingsley especially likes climbing indoors because "it is not as dangerous as climbing outdoors, you meet lots of nice people of all ages, and the routes are always really fun."

In the spring of 1994, Hans Florine had recently set a speed record on El Capitan's *Nose* route. One evening at City Rock, Melanie was joking around with Hans and said "You and Kingsley should climb the Nose!" Before long the lighthearted teasing became reality and Kingsley, Melanie, and Hans were packing up a haul bag.

Kingsley had much to say about their attempt at climbing the Nose:

"I didn't know exactly what I was getting into, and it was totally different than I thought it would be. I got really scared at one of the belay points and an anchor kept slipping and creaking - I thought it might come out! My mom helped to calm me down. I was most excited when I peaked my head over this tiny granite ledge and saw where I would be sleeping 2,200 feet off the ground! I was really tired from climbing for 17 hours, and finally fell asleep. I wasn't quite sure where I was when I woke up, but then I looked around and knew.

Kingsley Learner

"We were at Dolt Tower and it was obvious that we did not have enough water. We should have prepared for it better. At that point we made a decision to rappel to the ground and try again another time. I really hope I can try again and do it before I turn 13. Next time I will know what to expect and it will make it a lot easier for me."

Kingsley is proud of her achievement in climbing to Dolt tower, but she feels her personal best is her ability to help others. As far as climbing goes, she feels that her strong point is her flexibility, a trait which comes quite naturally to her. She participates in several activities including soccer, skiing, cheerleading for her school, and jazz dance. One of the best times she ever had climbing was at the Lollapalooza concert where they had a climbing wall set up. Kingsley noted a highlight from her experience: "There was a big buffed guy who couldn't get anywhere on the wall. I was able to walk right up the wall! Best of all though, my best friend got to see me climb."

Kingsley hopes to continue climbing and to enter more competitions. She wants to climb Half Dome and maybe try climbing professionally some day. She plans to be a therapist for children and hopes she can have a wall in her office so the kids can climb and talk and work out their problems.

Kingsley recommends climbing for people of any age:

"Everyone should definitely try climbing. Get lessons though, for safety and some tips on how to climb. You don't want to make safety mistakes!"

Finally, about her ascent of El Capitain to Dolt Tower:

"It was both the most exciting and the scariest thing I have ever done. I feel really honored to have had the opportunity to try the ascent. I can't wait to try again!"

Soledad Rosas

Soledad Rosas was born in 1984 with cerebral palsy. She has had several operations on her legs and continues to work hard at walking with cuff crutches or using a wheel chair. The first time she wheeled herself into Pacific Edge she was a bit timid to try climbing. With a little encouragement and a lot of determination she got into a harness and approached her first ascent.

"I thought climbing was so fun! I thought that I could do it and I did. It was hard sometimes for me because you have to use both your hands and feet at the same time to climb. I got pretty tired by the time I reached the top of the wall. It was amazing to get so high off the ground - I never thought I would do that! I thought that I might get frustrated climbing, but I didn't. It was really fun.

Soledad Rosas

"I hope that other people will try climbing. People with disabilities can do it too. If you think you can do something, you can. You can at least try to do it. I know that if I can climb a wall, others can do it too."

Climbing Games for Kids of All Ages

There are numerous activities Pacific Edge instructors commonly use to encourage young people to expand their notions about movement. These exercises are offered for you to experiment with; they can be a great way to warm up, train, and to have fun.

1. Climb wearing a blindfold - check all safety systems before hiding your eyes!

2. Climb using only one hand and two feet or only one foot and two hands.

3. Climb using only foot holds with your palms or fingertips for balance only.

4. Climb using only hand holds with your feet on the wall only.

5. Climb with a partner on the boulder. The climber follows the hand holds the person with the stick points out.

6. Follow the leader on the boulder. This can be done with a group of any size. See who gets further or who stays on the longest without falling off.

7. Climb in slow motion.

8. Speed climb.

9. Climb as many vertical feet as possible without stopping by climbing both up and down. Calculate the number of feet climbed.

10. Stop while you're still having fun!

Climbing Gyms In North America

Climbing gyms and recreational climbing walls have sprouted up all over the country, and the following is a partial list of those found in the United States and Canada. New gyms are opening every month; to find out if there is one in your area, check the telephone directory under "health clubs," refer to the back of magazines aimed at climbers, or telephone another gym and ask them. Here are a few tips for making the most out of your visit once you finally get there:

- Most gyms will allow visitors to view the climbing area of their facility at any time. If you are planning to climb at a facility for the first time, prepare yourself by calling ahead for information such as admission price, class days and times, cost of rental equipment, and hours of operation.

- Climbing gyms frequently hold special events or have parameters you should know about. CALL AHEAD to find out whether anything is going on the day you want to climb that might interfere with your plans.

- Be prepared to take a knot and belay test. If you are an experienced climber, the test shouldn't be a problem. If you are the friend of an experienced climber and he has taught you in five or ten minutes "everything you need to know," proceed with caution. Consider the responsibility you are taking on, and seriously consider if you would like to take a life into your own hands. Belaying is not difficult, but a thorough understanding is necessary, even when using a Grigri.

- If you are under 18, always assume you will need a parent or guardian to sign a waiver and release of liability form provided by the facility before you climb. If you can't bring a parent with you, have the gym mail you a waiver.

- Most climbing gyms are built in warehouses. They can be very cold or hot and often not in ideal locations. Because not every gym has a *Beckmann's Bakery & Bistro,* you may have to pack your own lunch.

- Be prepared to pay for use of the facility.

ALASKA
Alaska Pacific University
4101 University Drive
Anchorage, AK 99908 (907) 564-8303

Anchorage Gymnastics
525 West Potter #4
Anchorage, AK 99518 (907) 563-3041

Anchorage Rock Club
9641 Vanguard Suite 21
Anchorage, AK 99507 (907) 344-7607

ALABAMA
TLS, Inc.
P.O. Box 2646
Huntsville AL 35804 (205) 533-7025

ARIZONA
Jagged Edge
806 E. Sack
Phoenix AZ 85024 (602) 492-0902

Northern Arizona Rock
315 North Aqassiz
Flagstaff AZ 86001 (602) 779-5888

Rocks and Ropes
330 South Toole Ave. #450
Tucson, AZ 85701 (602) 882-5924

Phoenix Rock Gym
2810 South Roosevelt #101
Tempe, AZ 85285 (602) 921-8322

ARKANSAS
Fayetteville Rock Gym
347.5 North West Avenue
Fayetteville, AR 72701 (501) 582-2558

CALIFORNIA
Arete Climbing Park
14700 Oak Road
Los Gatos, CA 95030 (408) 255-5498

Atoll Holdings
Box 3259
San Luis Obispo, CA   93403 (805) 544-8203

City Rock
1250 45th Street Suite 400
Emeryville, CA 94608 (510) 654-2510

Class 5 Fitness
25 B Dodie Street
San Rafael, CA 94901 (415) 485-6931

Climb USA
4066 Stage Court Bldg. F.
Placerville, CA 95667 (916) 626-4284

Foot Trail
1341 Martin Lane
Placerville, CA 95667 (916) 622-1222

Humboldt State University Traversing Wall
Recreation Department Field House
Arcata, CA 95521 (707) 826-4536

Indoor Mountains
3120 Brasilia Court
Sacramento, CA 95826 (916) 366-6617

Pacific Edge
104 Bronson Street #5.12
Santa Cruz, CA 95062 (408) 454-9254

CityRock San Francisco
2295 Harrison Street
San Francisco, CA (415) 647-6800

Planet Granite
2901 Mead Avenue (off of Burrows)
Santa Clara, CA 95051 (415) 648-7523

Rock and Roll
26860 Jefferson Avenue #E
Murrieta, CA 92562 (909) 677-7430

Rockcreation Sport Climbing
1300 Logan Avenue
Costa Mesa, CA 92626 (714) 556-7625

Rocknasium
720 Olive Drive #Z
Davis, CA 95616 (916) 757-2902

SolidRock Gym
2074 Hancock Street
San Diego, CA 92110 (619) 299-1124

The Force
2603 Rockefeller Lane
Redondo Beach, CA 90278 (310) 374-3558

The Vertical Hold
9580 Distribution Ave.
San Diego, CA 92121 (619) 586-7572

UCSB Climbing Wall
Robertson Gym 2120
University of California Santa Barbara
Goleta, CA 93106 (805) 893-3737

COLORADO

Aspen Athletic Club
720 East Hyman Avenue
Aspen, CO 81611 (303) 925-2531

Boulder Rock Club
2952 Baseline Road
Boulder, CO 80303 (303) 447-2804

Breckenridge Recreation Center
880 Airport Road
Breckenridge, CO 80424 (303) 453-1734

CATS
2400 30th Street
Boulder, CO 80424 (303) 939-9699

Club Rock
P.O. Box 1237
Breckenridge, CO 80424 (303)453-0626

Colorado Mountain Sports
124 22nd.Ct. #C
GandJunction, CO 81501 (303)434-7697

Healthworks
415 East Monroe
Fort Collins, CO 80525 (303) 226-8786

Inner Strength Rock Gym
3713 South Mason
Fort Collins, CO 80525 (303) 282-8118

Mountain Mocks
P.O. Box 18872
Denver, CO 80218 (303) 894-8141

Paradise Rock Gym
6260 North Washington Street #5
Denver, CO 80216 (303) 286-8168

Rocky Mt. Forest & Range
240 West Prospect St.
Fort Collins, CO 80526 (303) 498-2128

The Point Athletic Club
53533 Van Gordon Street
Lakewood, CO 80525 (303) 988-1300

Sport Climbing Center
4650 Northpark Drive
Colorado Springs, CO 80918 (303) 260-1050

Steamboat Athletic Club
33250 Storm Meadows Drive
Steamboat Springs, CO 80487 (303) 879-1036

The Point Athletic Club
53533 Van Gordon Street
Lakewood, CO 80228 (303) 988-1300

Thrillseekers
1912 South Broadway
Denver, CO 80210 (303) 733-8810

Vail Athletic Club
352 East Meadow Drive
Vail, CO 81657 (303) 476-7960

Vertical Works
2845 Chipeta Avenue
Grand Junction, CO 81501 (303) 245-3610

Westminister Recreation Center
10455 Sheridan Blvd.
Westminister, CO 80020 (303) 879-1036

CONNECTICUT
Go Vertical!
Box 111413
Stamford CT 06911-1413 (203) 358-8767

Prime Climb
340 Quinnipiac Street Building 28
Wallingford, CT 06492 (203) 265-7880

Ragged Mountain Outdoor Center
195 Adams Street
Manchester, CT (203) 645-0015

Willimantic YMCA
Willmantic, CT (203) 423-2513

FLORIDA
Tampa Rock Gym
5019 Rio Vista Ave.
Tampa, FL 33634 (813) 887-3747

Weatherford's Climbing Wall
3009 East Cervantes
Pensacola FL 32503 (904) 469-9922

GEORGIA
The Sporting Club
135 Interstate North Parkway
Atlanta, GA 30339 (404) 953-1100

The Climb'n Shop
Box 301
Carrollton GA 30117 (404) 834-2100

HAWAII
Gecko Gym
Box 26202
Honolulu HI 96825 (808) 737-4472

IDAHO
Boise State University
1910 University Drive
Boise, ID 83725 (208) 385-1951

Wings Rock Gym
1875 Century Way
Boise, ID 83709 (208) 376-3641

ILLINOIS
Athletic Club Illinois
211 North Stetson Avenue
Chicago, IL 60601 (312) 616-9000

Climb Sport, Inc.
482 James Ct. Suite D
Glendale Heights IL 60139 (708) 469-9403

Gravity Rock Gym
1935 South Halsted
Chicago, IL 60608 (312) 733-5006

Hidden Peak at Lakeshore Academy
1780 N. Marcey Place
Chicago, IL 60614 (312) 335-1200

Midwest Rocksport
108 1st Street
Batavia, IL 60510 (708) 879-8889

Northwall Climbing Gym
824 South Main St.
Crystal Lakes, IL 60014 (815) 356-6855

Upper Limits
1220 37th Street
Peru, IL 61354 (815) 224-3686

Vertical Plains
25 East Springfield Avenue
Champaign, IL 61820 (217) 356-2412

Wheaton Park District
85 N. Gilbert
LaGrange, IL 60525

KENTUCKY
Climb Time
2416 Over Drive
Lexington, KY 40510 (606) 253-3673

Rocksport Inc.
3383 Freys Hill Road
Louisville, KY 40241 (502) 425-5884

MAINE
University of Maine
Memorial Union
Orono, ME 044469 (207) 581-1794

MARYLAND
Clipper City Rock Gym
2017 Clipper Park Drive
Baltimore, MD 21211 (410) 467-9727

Rockville Climbing Gym
805 Avery Road
Rockville, MD 20805 (301) 217-0525

MASSACHUSETTS
Boston Rock Gym
149 Highland Avenue
Somerville, MA 02143 (617) 776-8703

Central Branch YMCA
766 Main Street
Worcester, MA 01610 (508) 755-6101

MICHIGAN
Ann Arbor Climbing Gym
324 West Ann Street
Ann Arbor, MI 48104 (313) 761-4669

Alquin Group
100 Renaissance Suite
Detroit, MI 48243 (313) 259-0666

Benchmark
32715 Grand River Street
Farmington, MI 48355 (313) 477-8116

Footprints
2310 3rd St. NE
Minneapolis, MN 55418 (612) 788-1414

Inside Moves
639.5 76th Street West
Grand Rapids, MI 49509 (616) 281-7088

Peak Adventure
9208 James Ave. S #3
Bloomington, MN 55431 (612) 884-7996

Planet Rock Gym
34 Rapid Street
Pontiac, MI 48342 (810) 334-3904

Vertical Endeavors LLC
519 Payne Ave.
St. Paul, MN 55101 (612) 778-1975

MINNESOTA
Peak Adventure
9208 James Avenue South
Bloomington, MN 55431 (612) 884-7996

Vertical Endevours
844 Arcade Street
St. Paul, MN 55106 (612) 776-1430

MISSOURI
Ninth Street Gym
1720 11th Street
St. Louis, MO 63126 (314) 436-2633

RADZ Rock Gym
836 N. Glenstone
Springfield, MO 65804 (417) 881-1141

MONTANA
Don's Inc.
618 W. Main St.
Lewiston, MT 59457 (406) 538-4453

Pipestone Mountaineering, Inc.
829 South Montana Street
Butte, MT 59701 (406) 782-4994

NEW HAMPSHIRE
Cranmore Recreation Center
P.O. Box 1640
North Conway, NH 03860 (800) 786-6754

The Rock Barn
Arlyn Farms Route 25
Plymouth, NH 03264 (603) 536-2717

NEW JERSEY
Up The Wall
33 McGuire Street
East Brunswick, NJ 08816 (908) 249-2865

NEW MEXICO
Albuquerque Rock Gym
3300 Princeton NE #S-30
Albuquerque, NM 87107 (505) 881-3073

Duke City Sport Climbing Academy
2832 Girard NE
Albuquerque, NM 87107 (505) 884-6949

High Desert Rock Gym
825 Early Street #A
Santa Fe, NM (505) 989-7114

NEW YORK
ACC Gymnasium
Susquehanna Avenue
Cooperstown, NY 13326 (607) 547-2800

Albany's Indoor RockGym
4 C Vatrano Rd.
Albany, NY 12205 (518) 459-7625

City Climbing Club
533 West 59th Street
New York, NY10025 (212) 408-0277

Climb Manhattan
482 West 43rd Street
New York, NY 10036 (212) 563-7001

Extra Vertical
125 W. 96th St. #1D
New York, NY 10025 (212) 865-4383

Hard As A Rock
630 Glen Street
Queensbury, NY 12804 (518) 793-4626

Lindseth Climbing Wall
Cornell University, PO Box 729
Ithaca, NY 14851 (607) 255-1807

Long Island Rocks
1066 Merillon Ave.
Westbury, NY 11590 (516) 333-7960

Ocean Rock
3800 Veterans Highway
Bohemia, NY 11716 (516) 471-9500

Rockworks
1385 Vischer Ferry Road
Clifton Park, NY 12065 (518) 373-1215

Silver Bay Association
YMCA Conference Center
Silver Bay, NY 12874 (518) 543-8833

View Video
34 East 23rd St.
New York, NY 10010 (212) 674-5550

NORTH CAROLINA
Charlotte Climbing Center
619 S Cedar St.
Charlotte, NC 28022 (704) 333-7625

Climbax Sport
43 Wall St.
Asheville, NC 28801 (704) 252-8996

North Carolina State Univ.
P.O. Box 8111
Raleigh, NC 27695 (919) 515-1056

Sandhills Vertical Gym
P.O. Box 3789
Pinehurst, NC 28374 (910) 295-0724

TRIX Gymnastics
3711 Aliance Dr.
Greensboro, NC 27407 (910) 852-1882

Tumblewees
6904 Downwind Rd.
Greensboro, NC 27409 (910) 665-0662

OHIO
Cleveland Rock Gym
8414 West Craig Dr.
Chagrin Falls, OH 44023 (216) 543-2795

Climb Time
10898 Kenwood Road
Blue Ash (Cincinnati), OH (513) 891-4850

Miami University Climbing Wall
Oxford, OH 45056 (513) 529-2360

Vertical Adventures Rock Gym
Columbus, OH 43220 (614) 888-8393

OKLAHOMA
Oklahoma State University
Stillwater, OK 74075 (405) 744-5510

Summit at the Santa Fe Club
6300 North Sante Fe
Oklahoma City, OK 73118 (405) 842-7625

OREGON
Club Vertical
P.O. Box 1552
Winston, OR 97496

Entre Rrises USA, Inc.
550 NW Hill St.
Bend, OR 97701 (503) 388-5463

Portland Rock Gym
2034 SE 6th Street
Portland, OR 97214 (503) 232-8310

Stoneworks
6775 SW 111th Avenue
Beaverton, OR 97005 (503) 644-3517

PENNSYLVANIA
Base Camp
723 Chestnut Street
Philadelphia, PA (215) 592-7956

Climb North
P.O. Box 36
Wildwood, PA 15091 (412) 487-5999

Climb On
1206 North Sherman Street
Allentown, PA 18103 (215) 435-4334

Climbing Wall, Inc.
7501 Penn Avenue
Monroeville/Pittsburgh, PA 15208 (412) 247-7334

Climbnasium
Box 453
New Kingston, PA 17072 (717) 795-9580

Climbnasium
339 Locust Point Road
Mechanicsburg, PA 17005 (717) 795-9580

Exkursion
4123 Penn Highway
Pittsburgh, PA 15146 (412) 372-7030

Mountain Dreams International
1121 Bower Hill Road
Pittsburgh, PA 15243 (412) 276-8660

Philadelphia Rock Gym
422 Business Center
East 520 North Circle Drive
Oaks, PA 19456 (215) 666-7673

Stan Rescue Training
P.O. Box 1574
South Hampton, PA 18966 (215) 357-8637

The Climbing Wall, Inc.
7501 Penn Ave.
Pittsburgh, PA 15208 (412) 247-7334

RHODE ISLAND
Rhode Island Rock Gym
210 Weeden Street
Pawtucket, RI 02860 (401) 727-1704

SOUTH DAKOTA
Dakota Rock Gym
1830 Lombardy Drive
Rapid City, SD 57701 (605) 342-6542

TEXAS
Backwoods
5500 Greenville Ave.
Dallas, TX 75206 (214) 363-0372

Exposure Rock Gym
2389 B Midway Road
Carollton, TX (214) 732-0307

Friedkin Adventure Co.
13201 NW Freeway
Houston, TX 77040 (713) 744-5263

Stone Works Climbing Gym
1003 Fourth Avenue
Carollton, TX (214) 323-1047

Sun & Ski Sports
5503 FM 1960 West
Houston, TX 77069 (713) 537-0928

UTAH
Rock Garden
22 South Freedom Boulevard
Provo, UT 84601 (801) 375-2388

Rockcreation
Salt Lake City, UT (801) 278-7473

Wasatch Body Shop
1305 East Gunn Avenue
Salt Lake City, UT 84106 (801) 484-0873

Wasatch Front
427 West Universal
Sandy, UT 84070 (801) 565-3657

Worldwide Outfitter & Guides
1787 East Fort Union Blvd.
Salt Lake City, UT 84152 (801) 942-7863

VIRGINIA
Rocky Top Climbing Club
HC 1 Box 111
Earlysville, VA 22936 (804) 973-5884

The Wall at Body Works
500 Nelms Circle
Fredricksburg, VA 22406 (703) 899-9111

WASHINGTON
Cliff Hanger
200 Airport Way
E Wenatchee, WA 98802 (509) 884-9608

Climb Axe
301 W Holly St. #D25
Bellingham, WA 98225 (206) 734-8433

Evergreen State College
2129 Jackson Ave NW
Olympia, WA 98502 (206) 866-6000

Olympic Rock Gym
215 7th Ave.
Olympia, WA 98501 (206) 705-1585

The Vertical Club
15036-B NE 95th Street
Redmond, WA 98052 (206) 881-8826

The Vertical Club
1111 Elliot Avenue West
Seattle, WA 98119 (206) 283-8056

Wild Walls climbing Gym
45122 Lakeshore Homes
Loon Lake, WA 99148 (509) 233-8905

WEST VIRGiNIA
Wilderness Gallery
376 High Street
Morgantown, WV 26505 (304) 292-2777

WISCONSIN
Active Endeavors of Madison
341 State Street
Madison, WI 53703 (608) 257-8500

WYOMING
Club Energize
2701 South Douglas Highway
Gillette, WY 82718 (307) 686-7627

Gravity Club
555 Amoretti
Lander, WY 82520 (307) 332-6249

Teton Rock Gym
1116 Maple Way
Jackson, WY 83001 (307) 733-0707

CANADA
Captial City Rockhouse
#309-2040 York Ave.
Vancouver, BC V6J1E7 (604) 739-9217

Cliffhanger Indoor Rock
106 West 1st Ave
Vancouver, British V5Y 1A4 (604) 874-2400

Coyote Rock Gym
2000 Thurston Dr. #31
Ottawa ONT R1G4K7

Fundy Rock & Ice Climbing
P.O. Box 6713
St. John, New Bruns E2L4S2 (506) 632-8819

Gibraltar Rock Climbing Gym
175 Stronach, Crescent #D
London, ONT N5V 3G5   (519) 453-7625

Joe Hockhead's Gym
29 Fraser Avenue
Toronto, ONT M8Z 4N4 (416) 538-7670

Passe-Montagne
1760 Montee 2E Rang
Val-David, Quebec J0T 2N0 (819) 322-2123

Rock & Chalk
252 Church St.
Kewisk, Ontario L4P 1K1 (905) 476-3307

Toronto Climbing Academey
100 Broadview Avenue
Toronto, ONT M4M 3H3 (416) 406-5900

The Rock House
3771 Jacombs #520
Richmond, BC V6V 2L9 (604) 276-0021

The Edge
#2-1485 Velch Street
North Vancouver, BC V7P 1B5 (604) 984-9080

University of Alberta Climbing Wall
Outdoor Center PAV-153
Edmonton, Alberta (403) 429-2767

Project Climb
Incorporated

Mission

Project Climb is a non-profit organization which serves low income, "at risk," developmentally challenged, physically challenged, minority and needy young people between the ages of 12 to 17 by offering them climbing instruction, access to climbing facilities and equipment.

Philosophy

Learning the basic safety skills for climbing and the activity of climbing encourages mental, emotional, and physical development. The activity of climbing will challenge the student in ways he or she needs to be challenged. Project Climb provides an opportunity for young people to experience these benefits of climbing as they occur to the student.

Project Climb is not designed to be a "personal growth" program. Students involved in Project Climb are referred by teachers, counselors, or agencies who already work with the students to process aspects of their lives. Project Climb allows students the opportunity for emotional growth through climbing and leaves the question of how it applies to the participant's life for each individual to answer. Beneficial results include developing physical capabilities, increasing problem solving skills, raising self esteem, enhancing trust and a sense of responsibility.

Methods

While ensuring emotional and physical safety, Project Climb strives to allow students to learn through experience at their own pace. Students are encouraged to use their critical thinking skills to make them active rather than passive learners.

Students are encouraged to work together to solve problems for themselves. The opinions, suggestions, and comments of all students are treated with respect. Thus, "students are given opportunities for their voices to be heard, their actions to be recognized, and their positive impact to be felt" (Rebecca Carver, from "*What do Students Experience In Schools that are Based on Experiential Education?*").

For more information write to:
Project Climb
104 Bronson Street #12
Santa Cruz, CA 95062

Glossary

Active end of rope:
The end which leads to the climber from the belay device.

Active hand:
The belayer's hand which may move freely; not the brake hand.

Aid:
A form of climbing often used to ascend big walls; route setters at the gym often utilize aid techniques.

Always:
Something you do every time, like checking your safety systems.

Arete:
An outside corner of a wall.

Belay:
Friction system used to secure a climber.

Belay loop:
The part of the harness linking the leg loops to the waist belt, usually a sewn piece of webbing.

Beta:
As in VHS or BETA; slang for getting the scoop on anything related to climbing equipment, routes, climbers.

Bight:
Rope terminology for a bend in the rope.

Big wall:
As in Yosemite's big granite walls - often several thousand feet high, once climbed with aid exclusively. The Nose route on El Capitain is a classic Big Wall route.

Bolt:
A fixed anchor point used in climbing gyms and outdoors.

Bomb-proof:
Climber's slang for very safe.

Brake hand:
The hand used to stop the rope from passing through the belay device; it never leaves the rope.

Carabiner:
Metal 'snap links' with a spring loaded; some lock.

Careless:
The way climbers are just before an accident.

Communication:
What happens between the climber and the belayer prior to climbing and belaying; lack thereof may result in complications.

Crimper:
A small hand hold; edge.

Crux:
The most difficult move on a route.

Double-backed:
Most harnesses manufactured in America require thatt the webbing of the waist belt be passed through the buckle twice (double-backed) to be effective. Instructions are generally sewn onto the waist belt and must be followed exactly.

Follow-through:
The process of tracing a knot; the figure eight follow through knot consists of two parallel figure eight knots.

Grigri:
A type of belay device manufactured by Petzel; an effective charm used by voodoo practitioners.

Ground school:
Where safety skills for climbing are generally taught, in the horizontal realm rather than the vertical.

Harness:
The piece of equipment used to link the climber to the safety system. Harnesses must be used exactly as specified by the manufacturer to be effective.

Human:
Prone to error - doublecheck your safety systems!

Kernmantle:
A type of rope used for climbing.

Lead:
The first climber on a route; the climber who takes the rope with him
while securing into anchors points along the way.

Leg loops:
The part of the harness through which the legs pass. One of the tie-in
points of the harness may be through the leg loops.

Munther Hitch:
A type of rope hitch which may be used to belay; generally not an
approved method for belaying in the gym.

On-sight:
To climb a route without falls or weighting the rope and without prior
knowledge of the moves.

Pinkpoint:
To lead a route where the protection is already in place; most climbing
gyms with lead climbing are equipped with protection in place, hence
leads in gyms are generally pinkpoints.

Protection:
The anchore points used by lead climbers which may be fixed (like a
bolt) or removable (like a nut or camming device); the proverbial
piton.

Pumped:
The way one's forearms feel after climbing.

Quickdraws:
Two carabiners with a piece of webbing between them. Used in lead
climbing as points of protection when clipped into a bolt.

Rack:
The equipment you take with you climbing; virtually obsolete in the
gym.

Rappel:
A method of descent, generally not necessary in the climbing gym.

Sandbag:
Rating a climbing route easier than it really is.

Sharp end:
Slang for the lead end of the rope - sharp because a fall may hurt.

Sticky rubber:
The type of rubber which sets $150 climbing shoes from your $20
Converse high tops.

Top rope:
A type of climbing system in which the main anchor is at the top of the
wall.

INDEX

MOCK ROCK Newsletter

The *MOCK ROCK Newsletter* is a quarterly publication intended for anyone who is an avid indoor climber or is just getting into climbing. The newsletter features a Question & Answer section addressing questions from subscribers on nearly any topic concerning indoor and outdoor climbing. The MOCK ROCK newsletter also contains:

- climbing gym profile (interesting details about new gyms, or gym events, etc.)
- climbing news and information
- climbing equipment and product reviews
- people profiles

Feature articles put emphasis on topics aimed at beginning climbers, special focus on women and climbing, kids and climbing, 70's climbers who are now parents and taking their families to climbing gyms and getting back into climbing, and interesting articles for the new generation of climbers.

Special departments include:

- techniques and health
- family climb-time
- book reviews (related mountaineering, fitness, and literature - with emphasis on successful climbing endeavors written for general audiences).
- learning from Project Climb; focus on what works when working with young people, opportunities, and news.

One year subscription is only $12.50

Order Form

Please send me _____ copy(ies) of *MOCK ROCK: The Guide To Indoor Climbing* @ $12.95 each.

I wish to subscribe for _____ year(s) to the *MOCK ROCK Newsletter* @ $12.50 per annual subscription.

NAME:_____

ADDRESS:_____

Fill out form and send check or money order in U.S. funds. All payments made to:
PAPER CHASE PRESS
Send orders to:
PAPER CHASE PRESS
5721 Magazine St., Suite 152, New Orleans LA 70115
Add $1.80 shipping & handling for each book ordered in the U.S. ($4.00 for S&H outside U.S.). For orders in Louisiana, add 9% sales tax. Allow 4 to 6 weeks for delivery.